ENGLISH MEDIAEVAL
PAINTED GLASS

Other reissues by SPCK

English Churchyard Memorials   Frederick Burgess
Sundials: Incised Dials or Mass-Clocks   Arthur Robert Green

J. D. LE COUTEUR

ENGLISH MEDIAEVAL
PAINTED GLASS

SECOND EDITION
With the original illustrations

LONDON
S P C K

First published in the Historic Monuments of England series 1926
First paperback edition 1978
SPCK
Holy Trinity Church
Marylebone Road
London NW1 4DU

The text of this volume was revised and prepared for the press by Mr. G. McN. Rushforth, F.S.A., who also added a few notes in square brackets.

Printed in Great Britain by
Whitstable Litho Ltd., Whitstable, Kent

ISBN 0 281 03605 5

PREFACE

DESPITE the iconoclasm of the Protestant reformers of the sixteenth and seventeenth centuries, and the ignorance, carelessness, and indifference of incumbents and churchwardens during the eighteenth, nineteenth, and (it is regrettable to add) even of the twentieth centuries, a very large quantity of ancient painted glass still remains in the windows of our cathedrals and parish churches, together with lesser portions in some of our secular and domestic buildings. Although great and increasing interest is taken in the subject, there still seems to be no book that is really of help to the beginner.

Numerous works, both expensive and otherwise, have of course been written upon the subject, treating it from many different standpoints, and containing a vast amount of invaluable information. In some cases, however, the writers have dealt with continental glass, as well as English; in others they have written in such a technical manner as to bewilder the amateur student. For that reason, therefore, this book has been written. It endeavours to set out, from the very beginning, the history of English mediæval glass painting, treating it in a readable manner, avoiding unnecessary technicalities. Chapters have been included dealing with the mediæval glass painters themselves, religion in the Middle Ages, and its effect on contemporary art and subjects in mediæval windows; while for the first time the period 1350–1400 has been regarded as a separate phase in glass painting. The illustrations have also been selected with much care; a few plates of well-known windows have been included, but for the most part less familiar examples have been chosen, each thoroughly typical of the period or subject illustrated, yet without being hackneyed.

In conclusion, I wish to acknowledge the kindness and help so generously afforded by my many friends in the actual writing of the book. Especially do I owe the deepest gratitude to Mr. J. A. Knowles, F.S.A., and Mr. J. N. L. Myres for the invaluable assistance they have given me ; the former with Chapters I, II, and III, the latter with Chapters XII and XIII. I am also very deeply indebted to Messrs. D. H. M. Carter, A. Llewellyn-Smith, H. Llewellyn-Smith, and A. Snell, for all the valuable help that they have given me by collecting information upon important details, as it was required. Also to Mr. Herbert Chitty, F.S.A., Mr. F. H. Crossley, F.S.A., Mr. W. Marriott Dodson, Mr. Wilfrid Drake, Mr. F. C. Eeles, the Rev. Canon and Mrs. Goodman, the Very Rev. Dr. W. H. Hutton, Dean of Winchester, Mr. H. J. Moreton, Mr. Sydney Pitcher, Mr. G. McN. Rushforth, F.S.A., and Messrs. Frank and Harold Warren ; my very grateful thanks are due for their most generous help in various ways, either by furnishing information or by the loan of books.

For my illustrations I am deeply grateful to many friends, especially to Mr. F. H. Crossley, F.S.A., Mr. Wilfrid Drake, Mr. W. Marriott Dodson, the Rev. Canon Meyrick, Mr. Onslow, Mr. Sydney Pitcher, and Mr. Taunt. I desire also to express my gratitude to the authorities at the Victoria and Albert Museum.

JOHN DOLBEL LE COUTEUR.

NOTE

JOHN DOLBEL LE COUTEUR came of an old Jersey family, and was born on the island in 1883. Delicacy as a boy prevented him from being sent to a public school; and later his employment in a bank was brought to an end by a long illness, which left him incapacitated for continuous professional work. His active mind, however, sought for interests, and about 1904 he found one in the subject of mediæval painted glass, which was thenceforward to be his absorbing study. It was not based only on books and photographs, though by these means he gained a wide knowledge of English glass in districts beyond his reach. Far more valuable to him was personal observation, and with this object in view he moved about from place to place, and so became familiar with the glass of Canterbury, Exeter, Wells, Bristol, Fairford and the Cotswold district, Gloucester and Tewkesbury, Salisbury, and Oxford. Wherever he went he never lost an opportunity of making friends with, and learning from, the glass painters and glass specialists whom he came across, such as the late Mr. Maurice Drake of Exeter, and Mr. Sydney Pitcher of Gloucester. A later friendship was that of Mr. J. A. Knowles of York, to whose unequalled knowledge of the history and methods of glass-painting this volume owes much. A valuable experience was the chance offered during a stay at Great Malvern of following and helping in the releading of the larger part of the windows in the Priory Church.

During the War he volunteered for military service, but owing to his physical disabilities he had to be content with temporary employment in a bank at Portsmouth. When this ceased at the end of the War, he went to live at Winchester, and spent there the last years of his life—the most fruitful ones for his subject. He at once set to work to make a survey of all the old glass in the city, and the results were published in 1920 under the title *Ancient Glass in Winchester*, a work of permanent value, though (except for a paper on the great north transept window in Canterbury Cathedral contributed to *Archæologia Cantiana* in 1911) it was his first appearance in print. Here, in addition to a minute account of every scrap of ecclesiastical and domestic painted glass in the city and the Hospital of St. Cross, he told the story of the origin of the windows in the College Chapel, and of their later vicissitudes, as it had never been told before. In these researches he owed much to the sympathetic assistance of that sound antiquary, Mr. Herbert Chitty, the Bursar of Winchester College, whose example and methods were of the greatest value to him. At the same time he had access to the extensive private library of the Dean (the Very Rev. W. H. Hutton, D.D.), to whom he was now giving help in secretarial work; and, altogether, the larger world with which he was now in contact helped to mature his judgment and widen his knowledge. It was due to his close friendship with the Dean that he generously undertook the supervision of the work of releading and rearranging the mediæval glass in the great west window and elsewhere in the Cathedral during 1921; and the results were so successful that later the governing body of Winchester College entrusted him with the direction of the work of releading the windows of the College Chapel.

He was also indefatigable in searching out and reporting on old glass in Hampshire churches, and in this way he was of great use to the Diocesan Advisory Committee, as well as being instrumental in safeguarding remains which were sometimes of historical interest. Much of the last year of his life was spent in the composition of the present volume, and he was at work on it up to the end. He died on August 13, 1925.

It is astonishing that under such apparently unfavourable conditions Le Couteur reached the position of an authority in his subject, so that a writer (F. C. E.) in *The Guardian* of August 21, 1925, could say that his death deprived the country of one of the very few men with a really first-hand knowledge of the history and technique of English glass painting. It was achieved in the first place by his unusual power and accuracy of observation, and next by his determination to get at the truth. Though he was without a scholar's training, he took the utmost pains to ascertain the real facts in such matters as iconography and inscriptions on glass; and the spirit in which he worked was scientific. But he not only made himself master of his subject: he had the power, as well as the desire, of making it interesting to others; and this was due not only to the clearness of his mind, but also to the transparent candour and amiability of his character.

One of the happiest episodes of his life at Winchester was his intimate relations with the boys of the College through their Archæological Society. To quote one who writes with inside knowledge : " His ardent enthusiasm, his sense of humour and inexhaustible good nature, endeared him to generation after generation of young archæologists, among whom he made, and kept to the end, many real friendships. He had an absorbing zeal for arriving at the truth; and his influence on the minds of those with whom he came in contact was correspondingly profound." Another witness says : " He made the glass a live thing for the boys " ; and when the work of releading the Chapel windows was being carried out in " Old Mill " in the College grounds, many of the scholars took the keenest interest in the process, constantly visiting the workshop, and being encouraged to make suggestions. With one of them, Mr. D. H. M. Carter, we may add, he wrote for the *Antiquaries' Journal* (October 1924) an account of their discovery and reconstruction of the fragments of the shrine of St. Swithin in the Cathedral.

This brief memoir may be fitly concluded by some words spoken by the Dean at his funeral in the Cathedral. " To know him was to admire and love him. All his friends know how nothing he could do to help them was too great, nothing (which is a much rarer thing among friends) too little, for him to do : all the time so modestly, so loyally, so generously. He had those three qualities which, with the love and blessing of God, always make for a happy life : intellectual curiosity, a sense of fun, and a sense of duty. Those three keep us really ' alive ' through a hard or sad experience, and keep us young to the last."

G. McN. R.

CONTENTS

xii

CONTENTS

LIST OF ILLUSTRATIONS
In text

Between pages 80 and 81

xiii

ENGLISH MEDIÆVAL PAINTED GLASS

CHAPTER I

INTRODUCTORY

ANYTHING more than a glance at a coloured window will show that it consists of a mosaic of numerous pieces of coloured glass held together by strips of lead joined with solder, and that the various details were mostly obtained by drawing on the glass with an opaque pigment (coloured paint is never used) which has been burned into the surface by being baked in a white-hot oven.

The expression " stained glass " so often applied to coloured glass, whether mediæval or modern, is misleading and erroneous. It should be " painted glass." The earliest example of the use of the more popular term seems indeed to date only from 1752, when William Peckitt of York advertised himself as " a glass painter and stainer." [1] As a matter of fact, the only colour that could be imparted to glass by *staining* was yellow ; that is, apart from the coloured enamels introduced in the sixteenth century (see Chapter XI). It was discovered early in the fourteenth century that if white glass were painted with a liquid containing silver, and then baked in a hot oven, it would turn yellow, and that the shade could be made to

---

[1] *Notes and Queries*, October 22, 1921 : " Glass Painters of York : William Peckitt," by J. A. Knowles. [Perhaps W. Peckitt's description may have been suggested by the old trade title of " painter (and) stainer." The earliest instance given in the *New English Dictionary* (vol. ix, p. 775) is from Mrs. Radcliffe's *Romance of the Forest* (1791). *The Farington Diary* of November 23, 1793 (vol. i, p. 18), mentions " the stained glass " then being executed for St. George's Chapel, Windsor. Horace Walpole regularly uses " painted glass."]

vary from lemon to deepest orange, according to the quantity used, and to the length of time allowed for its baking. The imitation ruby glass of the eighteenth century, indeed, was all obtained by the use of stain, the process in this case simply consisting of repeated applications of liquid silver to a piece of white glass, each with its own " firing."

The discovery of yellow stain was of enormous importance to the mediæval glass painter. Prior to its invention he had to chip into shape pieces of yellow glass for any detail such as a crown, a mitre, or the head of a crozier. But once the properties of this new method came to be fully understood, the designer could, and eventually did, paint a head with halo, hair, and headgear all upon the same piece of white glass (Fig. 1), introducing yellow where required, and so saving himself a vast amount of labour, besides adding greatly to the beauty of the work that he produced.

The mediæval glassmaker made his glass by mixing sand, lime, and potash made from the ashes of plants or of seaweed, and melting them together in clay pots in a furnace. When white-hot, these ingredients fused together, making a liquid glass, and as they melted and sank down, more of the mixture was shovelled in, until the pot was full of liquid white glass, the scum which rose to the surface being skimmed off from time to time. The furnace was then allowed to cool down until the liquid glass " metal," as it was always called, became thick enough to be dealt with as required.

The tone of the white glass varied very greatly, that of the south being as a rule much greener in tone than that used by the northern glass painters. Much of the York glass is as near pure white as possible ; and even when it has a coloured tinge, the hue is yellowish rather than green. This greenish tone, which was due to the presence of iron in the sand with which the glass was made, could be eliminated to a certain degree by the intro-duction of a very little oxide of manganese into the pot.

The furnace used for the purpose of glass making was, as a rule, a circular, dome-shaped erection, constructed of clay, and divided into three tiers, each provided with apertures (Fig. 2). The lowest of these tiers contained the fire, the second the pots of glass, the topmost being used for " fritting," that is to say, subjecting the raw materials used in glass making to a preliminary roasting, until they formed a semi-vitrified mass which could be shovelled out and left in lumps or broken up prior to being placed in the pots. The fuel consisted of logs, which were piled up in heaps, so that during the process of melting (" founding," as it was termed) boys could run round, throwing in a billet of wood each time, thus keeping the furnace as hot as possible.

Coloured glass was obtained by mixing various metallic oxides with the materials used for making white or rather colourless glass. Thus copper oxide produced ruby; oxide of cobalt mixed in the pot produced blue. Oxide of iron was used for making green, the hue ranging from apple-green to deep green, or, in another proportion, yellow of a strong brassy tone. Soot or sulphur was also used for the purpose of making yellow glass; all these as apart from the " stained " yellow produced by the chloride of silver process. Oxide of manganese produced purple glass, a separate pot or crucible being of course used for every colour. These oxides were found in an impure state, and used in very much the same condition; consequently there was no certainty of tint. This amply accounts for the wide range of hues of any given colour found in mediæval glass.

The glass was made into small sheets technically termed " tables." The workman began by dipping the end of a metal blowpipe into a pot of molten glass and collecting a lump on to the end of it. He then blew the lump out into a bladder-shaped bubble, swinging it until it stretched by its own weight into a long bottle shape (Fig. 3). The top and the bottom

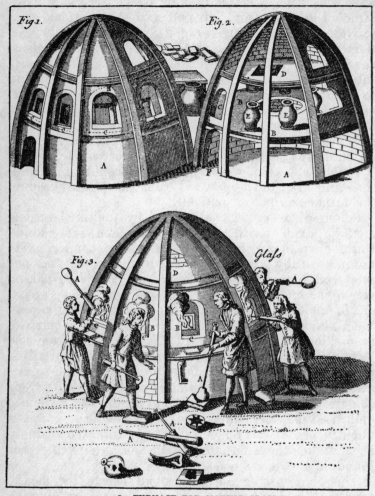

FIG. 2.—FURNACE FOR MAKING GLASS.
From a print in the *Dictionarium Polygraphicum* (2nd ed., London, 1758), vol. i, pl. xix, but based on older designs.

4

were then cut off to form a long cylinder, which was split down the side with a hot iron, and opened out after being re-heated in another furnace. The sheet so formed averaged about 24 inches by 15 inches, but varied considerably in thickness. This was known as the " muff " process. Another method of making tables of glass, equally popular in the Middle Ages, was to transfer the bubble, when blown out, to an iron rod, and then, having first cut a hole at the other end of the glass, to spin and whirl the rod between the workman's hands until at last the " bubble " opened out into a circular sheet some 24 inches in diameter. " Tables " produced by this method were known as " crown " glass. Whether a sheet of glass has been made by the " crown " or by the " muff " process can generally be detected from the direction of the bubbles. If these run in straight lines parallel with one another, the glass is " muff "; if, however, they run in ever-widening circles round a centre like ripples on the surface of water after a stone has been thrown in, the glass is " crown."

All coloured glass was divided into two classes : " pot-metal," and " flashed " or coated glass. The former, such as blue or green, was coloured throughout; the latter was white with a thin film of another colour. At first only ruby glass was treated in this manner, as pure pot-metal ruby was too opaque to admit light. The glass makers, finding that this red, which was of a very brilliant and beautiful tone, was too dense if pure, invented a method whereby white glass could be coated with ruby, and so obtained a transparent ruby. The method was to dip the iron blowpipe first into molten ruby glass, and having started a bubble, to dip it two or three times into white until a fair-sized lump had been collected. The bubble was then blown out and opened, with the result that a sheet of white was obtained, coated on one side with a thin film or " flash " of ruby. At first this method produced a very streaky and uneven glass, but as time went on and methods improved, the workers were able to make this flashed glass much thinner, and so more brilliant and even to work with. It was not until the sixteenth century that first a coated blue, and then a coated green, made their appearance, but neither seems even then to have been in much demand.

After yellow stain had been discovered, and its properties had become generally known, the glass workers found that they could obtain beautiful effects by scratching away this thin film from pieces of ruby or blue glass with an iron tool, and then, by staining yellow the exposed surface or parts of it, could obtain several colours upon one piece of glass. This method was termed " abrading and staining."

Prior to late in the sixteenth century only white glass was made in England, Chiddingfold in Surrey being a great place of manufacture. All the white glass used for the windows of St. Stephen's Chapel at Westminster (finally destroyed by fire in 1834 after having been used to accommodate the House of Commons), together with much of that required for windows at Windsor, was purchased from John de Alemaygne of Chiddingfold during the years 1351–56, the price paid varying from 6*d*. to 9*d*. per " ponder " or " wey " (5 lb. weight).[1] On the other hand, all coloured glass, and for that matter much white glass also, was made on the Continent, and imported into England. It is true that about the middle of the fifteenth century (1449) King Henry VI granted a patent of monopoly to one John Utynam, a Flemish glass manufacturer, " to make glass of all colours for the windows of Eton College " and King's College, Cambridge, adding that " the said art has never been used in England."[2]   But

[1] *Victoria County History of Surrey*, vol. ii, p. 296, quoted in Salzmann's *English Industries of the Middle Ages*, p. 128.

[2] *Transactions of the Society of Glass Technology*, vol. vi (1922): J. A. Knowles, " Processes and Methods of Mediæval Glass Painting," p. 257. The original grant to Utynam in the Record Office is reproduced by Mr. Knowles in *Glass*, vol. i (1924): " The Coloured Glass used in Mediæval Windows," p. 203. [See also vol. iii. (1926), pp. 157 ff.]

this experiment seems to have been a failure, as nothing more is heard of it.

There were two principal sources of supply of coloured glass in mediæval times : that of the North, comprising the glass-manufacturing districts of Hesse and Lorraine, and that of the South, viz. Normandy and Lower Burgundy. The glass of the former district was made in the forests on the banks of the upper reaches of the Weser, the Rhine and its tributaries, the Moselle, and the Maas or Meuse, and was conveyed down the rivers by raft or boat, ultimately reaching seaports such as Antwerp and Bruges. Hence this glass was generally known as " Reynyshe " (Rhenish) glass. It was imported into England through such ports as Hull or Bridlington, by the Merchant Adventurers and by the Hanse Merchants, the latter a powerful company of German merchants and traders, whose principal English office and place of business, the " Steelyard," as it was popularly termed, was situated in Thames Street in the City of London. Thus in the *Fabric Rolls of York Minster* such entries occurred as : " To Peter Faudkent, ' Dochman,' for glass of various colours bought at Hull from him this year with carriage," and " To John Ekworth of Bridlington for one wey of glass." [1]

The glass of the southern glass-making districts of Normandy and Lower Burgundy was similarly made on the upper reaches of the Seine with its tributary the Marne, and the Loire, and brought down to Rouen and similar inland ports, whence it could be exported to the southern ports of England. To take but one example, the glass, both white and coloured—that is, the raw, unpainted material—used for the windows of Exeter Cathedral early in the fourteenth century was all purchased at Rouen, the white at 6*d.* per foot, and the coloured at 1*s.* per foot. It was shipped to Sutton (the ancient name for the port of Plymouth)

---

[1] *Fabric Rolls of York Minster* (Surtees Society, vol. xxxv, 1858), pp. 69, 78. The writer is greatly indebted to Mr. J. A. Knowles of York for much of the above information.

and then reshipped to Exeter.[1] It was thus a matter
of convenience for the northern glass painters to use
Rhenish glass for their work, and for the southern
men to prefer French glass. Occasionally, however,
there were exceptions, for Sir John Petty, an eminent
glass painter of York, bequeathed " vj tabyls " (6
tables) " of Normandy white glasse " to the Dean and
Chapter of York Minster[2] ; while the coloured glass
used for the windows of St. Stephen's Chapel, Westminster, was all purchased from the London offices
of the Hanse Merchants in Thames Street, whence it
was sent by river to Westminster. The prices paid
for raw coloured glass varied very considerably. The
blue glass purchased for the windows of St. Stephen's
Chapel cost 1s. and also 3s. 7½d. per " ponder," while
" azure " glass cost 3s. per ponder. On the other hand,
four ponders of " safir " (sapphire) glass intended for
the windows of the Chapter House at Windsor Castle
only cost 3s. The ruby glass for St. Stephen's Chapel,
Westminster, cost 2s. 2d. per ponder.[3]

It should be noted that ancient glass differed considerably both in thickness and in density of colour.
That made in the twelfth and thirteenth centuries
was almost invariably very thick and uneven. Pieces
of white glass of this date if held in the hand become
almost opaque, mere dirty scraps of horn-like material,
while coloured glass of these periods when handled
resembles pieces of thin broken earthenware or glazed
tiles rather than glass. The glass of the fourteenth
century, especially the coloured material, varied considerably in thickness, but, generally speaking, showed
a greater tendency to smoothness than anything pre-

---

[1] Bishop and Prideaux, *The Building of Exeter Cathedral* (Exeter, 1922),
p. 50.

[2] *Testamenta Eboracensia*, vol. iv (Surtees Society, 1869), p. 334. The
writer again desires to thank Mr. J. A. Knowles for this information.

[3] [For the glass in St. Stephen's Chapel, see J. T. Smith, *Antiquities
of Westminster*, pp. 191-6 ; Brayley and Britton, *History of the Ancient
Palace of Westminster*, p. 176. For Windsor, see W. H. St. John Hope,
Windsor Castle, vol. i, p. 141.]

viously manufactured. The fifteenth century brought further changes, for the makers now produced coloured glass of a much thinner quality, though the white glass continued to be thick, and often retained its greenish tone until quite late in the century. Glass of the sixteenth century, both white and coloured, was almost invariably thin and smooth in texture, while the greenish tone of the former had practically disappeared.

It will be noticed that the exterior surface of ancient glass is often covered by a white chalky film, as though smeared over by a thin coat of whitewash. This was caused by the action of the elements upon the alkaline substances, such as the wood ashes of which the glass was partly composed. Rain, for instance, would gradually penetrate into little surface irregularities, dissolving the softer parts of the glass and eating its way into the interior, until the piece in question finally lost its transparency and was reduced to a disintegrated mass, whilst its inner surface would be coated with the lime washed out of it. This disintegration by corrosion is indeed one of the greatest dangers to which ancient glass can be exposed, for there is no protection against it. Contrary to popular belief, corrosion is not a sign of age in glass. It attacks badly made modern glass just as readily. Indeed, the glass of the twelfth and thirteenth centuries was so well and carefully made that in many cases it has defied corrosion, and is as sound as the day that it was put up. It was not until the fourteenth century that badly made glass began to appear in church windows. This was due, no doubt, to the increased demand for this form of decoration, and to the insufficient number of experienced glass makers, who, in common with every other class of society, had been decimated by the ravages of the Black Death in 1349–50. From this period onwards until about 1420, glass, especially ruby and blue, showed a marked tendency to corrode ; but after that it gradually improved again in quality, although now of much thinner texture than that of earlier centuries.

CHAPTER II

THE MAKING OF A PAINTED GLASS WINDOW

In order to make a coloured glass window, the mediæval craftsman (having first obtained the necessary measurements and taken "templates" or patterns of the various openings to be filled) began by making a drawing on a whitewashed board set up on trestles (Fig. 4). Lead or charcoal was used to sketch in the outline, the details of the flesh portions being painted in with red or brown, and the lines of the lead drawn over with a brush. This at least was the procedure prior to the use of parchment or paper on which the cartoon could be drawn. Even then some firms preferred the old-fashioned tables. At Westminster Palace, for instance, as late as 1351, six men termed "master glaziers" (the task of drawing the cartoon was usually carried out by the principal of the firm employed) were each paid 1s. per day for "drawing of the images, drawing and painting on white tables several images for the windows."[1] The tables were given a fresh coating of whitewash after each window or panel had been completed.

It is uncertain how much of the responsibility for the design itself was left to the firm employed. In many cases, no doubt, the donor contented himself with indicating the subjects to be placed in a window, or series of windows, leaving the actual designing, etc., to the firm employed. This seems to have been the method adopted in the cases of the Beauchamp Chapel, Warwick, King's College Chapel, Cambridge, and Henry VII's Chapel in Westminster Abbey. In

[1] Brayley and Britton, *Ancient Palace of Westminster*, p. 179.

10

the last-named example the King himself directed
in his will, drawn up in 1509, that " the windowes of
our said Chapell be glased, with stores [stories], ymagies,
armes, bagies [badges], and cognoisaunts, as is by us
redily divised, and in picture delivered to the Priour
of saunct Bartilmeus besids Smythfeld, maister of the
Works of our said Chapell."[1]   In this case the clerestory
was filled with the series of scriptural types and anti-
types, known as " the Story of the Olde Lawe and the
Newe " (see Chapters V and XI) ; the great west window
may have contained canopied figures of Apostles,
Prophets, and perhaps of the Nine Orders of Angels[2] ;
while the lower side-windows were filled with the
" armes, bagies, and cognoisaunts " set upon quarry
fields, the whole being in place by 1515.

In other cases the donor himself not only chose the
subjects, but drew up very precise instructions as to
the manner in which they were to be depicted, as witness
the following extract from a document of the time of
Henry VII, giving directions for the glazing of windows in
the Grey Friars' Church at Greenwich.[3]   It will be sufficient to quote the instructions for three figures only.

" Seint Edward Kyng of Englonde and Confessor
lying at Westminster sonne to Kyng Ethelberte.   Make
hym in the abbytt of a ryall peasible Kyng with a
berde [beard] of the age of iii[xx] yere [threescore] ; in
hys left honde a septure, a ball wyth a crosse thereon and
a ryng in his ryght honde and a crowne inperiall closse.
" His armys the felde asure a crosse golde v martletts
golde.
" Seint Edmond Kyng of Norffolke Suffolke and Essex

---

[1] This part of the will is printed in Neale's *History and Antiquities
of the Abbey Church of Westminster*, vol. i, p. 8.
[2] The figure of Jeremiah in the east window holds a composite scroll
reading: " Patrem laudate nomen domini."   The " Patrem " forms
part of the text usually held by this prophet (see page 45) ; the rest
may once have read : " (O Angeli) laudate nomen domini " (" O ye angels,
praise ye the name of the Lord ").   The figure itself has been cut down to
fit its present situation.
[3] Hasted's *History of Kent*, edited by H. H. Drake, part i, " The Hundred
of Blackheath " (London, 1886), p. 86, note 6.

martir lying at Bury in Suthefolke. Make hym in
thabbytte ryall of a peasible Kyng wyth a berde, an
arrowe in the ryghte hande a septure in the left hande
and an opyn crowne, his armys the felde asure iii crownes
of golde.

"Seint Audry a Kynges doughter shryned at Ely,
make her in thabbyte of a nonne wyth an opyn crowne
crowned, wyth a croyse in her ryghte honde a booke
in the left honde, a mantill of her armes. Her armys
the felde gowlis [gules, ruby] and iii crownes of golde."

As soon as the cartoon had been completed, the glass
was laid on the table and broken and chipped into the
required shapes. To accomplish this, the workman
first touched a piece of the glass with a hot iron, and
then dropped a little water on the heated place, and so,
having started a crack, continued it until he had divided
the glass into two portions. He then set to work to
chip one of these smaller pieces into the desired shape,
using for that purpose a little notched implement
termed a " groisour," " croysour," or " grozing-iron "
(see Fig. 9), which was described by Theophilus, a
twelfth-century writer on glass painting (see Chapter
III, p. 22), as being " a palm long and bent back at
each end," [1] and which left a nibbled edge rather resembling that made by a mouse's teeth. This part of the
work was carried out by a different set of men, who
received lower wages than the master glaziers. For
instance, at St. Stephen's, Westminster, twenty-four
men were each paid 6d. a day for " cutting and joining
the glass, joining and laying the glass, breaking and
joining the glass on the painted tables."

It should be added here that the diamond, which was
not introduced as a means of cutting glass until the
seventeenth century, leaves a perfectly smooth edge,
so that in releading ancient glass it is always possible
to ascertain whether it has been tampered with or
releaded since it was first put up.

[1] C. Winston, *Hints on Glass Painting*, 2nd ed. (Oxford and London,
1867), i, p. 369.

After all breaking and shaping was completed, the work of painting the glass began. This part of the work, again, was carried out by a different set of men, who in status ranked next to the master glaziers. At Westminster Palace fifteen workmen were each paid 7*d*. a day for "drawing on the glass." The pieces of glass were "laid on the table each in their proper place within marked-out leadlines, and the details such as eyes, nose, mouth, folds of drapery, inscriptions, and so forth, were painted in outline with vitrifiable pigment, being afterwards shaded with thin washes of the same pigment. This vitrifiable enamel was only intended to block out the light in varying proportions and so obtain shading. It had therefore to be opaque. Also it was necessary to use a pigment which would vitrify at a lower temperature than would be required to melt the glass on which it was painted. The enamel consisted of two parts of metallic oxide of copper or of iron, mixed with a soft glass ground to a fine powder and known as 'flux.' When exposed to the action of fire, this 'flux' melted and attached the opaque pigment to the surface of the glass." [1]

The actual painting was done by means of brushes made of hog's hair, or badger's hair. The mediæval craftsmen seem generally to have worked with their glass on the table, and not raised on easels, as is the case to-day.

All painting and, when it was discovered, staining having been completed (and in the Middle Ages only one coating was required, as against the two or three coatings of to-day), the glass was "fired." This seems to have been carried out as follows. A series of twigs were bent into the shape of an arch, and the ends stuck in the ground. Upon this foundation clay mixed with horse-dung and chopped hay was placed to the thickness of 3 or 4 inches, forming, as it were, a little tunnel, and in this the glass was "fired" on an

---

[1] *Journal of the Society of Glass Technology* for 1922, pp. 255–74: "Processes and Methods of Mediæval Glass Painting," by J. A. Knowles.

iron tray filled with whitening and raised sufficiently off the ground to allow of a fire being kindled beneath (Fig. 5).[1]   A later method of " firing " was to place

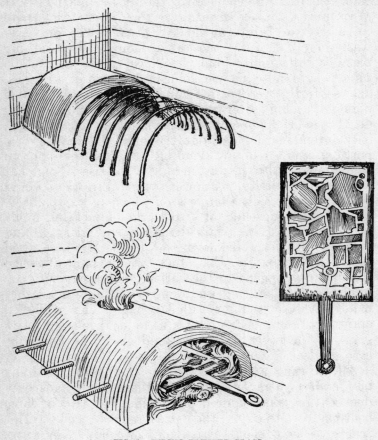

FIG. 5.—FIRING PAINTED GLASS.
From drawings by Mr. J. A. Knowles.

the glass in an iron pan filled with alternate layers of glass and of whitening and to bake it over hot coals.
    When all " firing " had been completed, and the

[1] " Processes and Methods of Mediæval Glass Painting," by J. A. Knowles, p. 267.

glass had been allowed to cool down again, the various pieces were laid out in their proper order on the tables and joined together by pieces of grooved lead termed " calmes " or " cawmes " (from the Latin *calamus,* a reed). These grooved leads were cast by laying a number of twigs or reeds (hence the name) in a shallow box, and then pouring molten lead round and over them. When cool, the lead was cut into thin strips and the twigs extracted, the result being a small lead of ⊥ shape (in profile), its length depending upon that of the reeds or twigs used. Another method of making " calmes " was to cast the lead in long thin moulds, and then to scrape grooves out of the thin bars so formed. The milled lead now in use was not invented until the seventeenth century, and when first brought into use was frequently made by running it through a mill stamped with the glass painter's name.

FIG. 6.—NAILING AND LEADING PAINTED GLASS ON THE TABLE.

From Salzmann's *Mediæval English Industries,* by permission of the Clarendon Press.

In order to keep the glass steady on the table during the process of " leading," the craftsman knocked in nails against the edges of the various pieces, pulling them out and knocking them in again farther on, as the work progressed (Fig. 6). These nails were termed " closying " nails (Fig. 9); the men who performed the task of leading up the glass being sometimes termed " clorours and joynours." When all leading was finished, the panel was surrounded by a double-lead band to give it strength. The pieces were then soldered together with a drop of solder at every join of the lead work, the solder used being a mixture of lead and tin melted together and poured into grooves on a board to bring it to stick-shape. Finally, a cement-like preparation was rubbed into the grooves of the lead to make the panel water-tight, broad strips of lead being soldered on to the panels to fasten them to the supporting bars. A light or opening in a window, if of large size, was made up of several panels.

In order to support the glass and make it less liable to be blown in by the wind, it was necessary to protect it internally by a grid of iron bars, both horizontal and vertical, the latter being termed " standards " (stanchions), the former " sondlets " (saddle-bars).

As might be expected, windows so constructed, and held together by such comparatively weak lead work, were liable to be blown in or otherwise damaged. For this reason, the mediæval glass painter was often called upon to repair windows, sometimes of much earlier date than his own period. In such cases he had either to make new panels, or insert new glass to match as best he could the older work both in colour and technique. Thus at Exeter Cathedral, one Robert Lyen, a glazier of that city, undertook in 1389 to design several new panels for the recently enlarged great east window of the choir, and, for the sake of preserving uniformity as far as possible, deliberately copied the stiff archaic " Decorated " canopy work and running foliate borders of the earlier glass painted for the smaller window more than sixty years before.[1] Again, at Winchester College the chapel windows, filled in 1393 with rich coloured glass at the cost of the Founder, William of Wykeham, Bishop of Winchester from 1367 to 1404, were constantly being repaired. For instance, the College Rolls record that in 1457 one Stephen Glasyer was called in to mend " 2 panels of the great east window [filled with a Tree of Jesse] in which are figures of Amos and Samuel the prophets," for which with some other minor work he was paid 3s. 8d.[2]

[1] Bishop and Prideaux, *The Building of Exeter Cathedral*, pp. 151-5.
[2] J. D. Le Couteur, *Ancient Glass in Winchester* (Winchester, 1920), p. 65.

Or, to quote one more example, John Prudde of Westminster, who from 1440 to 1461 held the responsible post of King's Glazier (see Chapter III, p. 29), carried out sundry minor repairs to windows at Greenwich Palace. These included " two heads of Virgins broken " at 12*d*. each ; also 6*d*. each for " two vestments, one of a Bishop the other of a Virgin." [1]

As noted above, the early use of whitened tables on which the designs for windows were drawn was superseded at a later date by cartoons drawn on parchment or paper. For example, the money expended on the enlargement in 1389 of the great east window of Exeter Cathedral included 2*d*. for a sheet of parchment on which the new work was to be designed. Or, again, the designs for the glass intended for the new chapel at Westminster Abbey, as the Founder-King Henry VII provided in his will, dated 1509, were to be " delivered in picture to the Prior of St. Bartholomew's Smithfield, Master of the Works of our said Chapel."

As the result of this improvement in method it was found possible to use the same cartoon over and over again, merely changing minor details, such as the position of hands, or the emblems held by figures, and of course varying the colour of robes or episcopal vestments. Thus in Great Malvern Priory Church the middle window of the north choir clerestory contains, amongst other personages, the figures of six bishops or archbishops, all produced from one cartoon, which, after serving as a design for four figures, was turned over, and with a few minor changes was made to do duty twice more. [2]

Another good example of this practice occurs in the famous " St. William " window of York Minster,

[1] Hasted, *History of Kent* (ed. Drake) : " Hundred of Blackheath," p. 56, note.

[2] The writer desires to thank Mr. J. A. Knowles for calling his attention to this detail. [See now his paper on " Mediæval Methods of Employing Cartoons for Stained Glass," in the *Journal of the British Society of Master Glass Painters*, No. 3 (October 1925), p. 35.]

given about the year 1421 by the De Roos family of
Helmsley Castle, Yorkshire. One panel shows a
mother who has brought her sick child and propped
him up against the shrine of the saint, while she prays
for his recovery. A spectator points with forefinger
at the child (Fig. 7). A second panel, closely modelled
upon the first, shows a leper woman cured at the shrine
(Fig. 8). Comparison of the two panels clearly shows
that the same cartoon has been used for each, but
that in the second the figure of the child having been
eliminated, the spectator in the background now points
at nothing at all." [1]

It is thus often possible to identify the work of some
particular firm as occurring in two different churches
many miles apart, even though the settings or backgrounds of the individual figure may differ entirely.
To take but one example. In the west window of
Cirencester Church in Gloucestershire is a late fifteenth-
century figure of St. Catherine, removed in 1796 from
some other window. The saint is shown as wearing
a mantle over an ermine cotehardie, holding her emblems
of sword and wheel, and standing on black and white
tiles, with a background of white and gold brocade.
At Oddingley Church in the adjacent county of Worcestershire a figure of the same saint appears in the
east window, which is identical in treatment of dress
and emblems, but placed this time upon a background of quarries, that is, of lozenge-shaped pieces
of white or greenish-white glass each painted with
some foliage device in matt and stain. It is evident
therefore that in this case the same firm had supplied
glass to both churches, but possibly for reasons of
expense had varied the background in the Oddingley
window.

It is a popular fallacy that the mediæval glass painter
was a sentimentalist, a man of high ideals, who worked

[1] *The Architects' Journal*, August 29, 1923 : " The York School of Glass
Painting," by J. A. Knowles. Also printed in the *Journal of the British
Archæological Association*, October 1923.

chiefly for the love of God's Church and its adornment, and to that end was content to labour for very small wages. In reality this was far from being the case, for "the mediæval craftsman was not called a man of craft for nothing! He had no more conscience than a plumber, and his knowledge of ways that are dark and tricks that are vain was extensive and peculiar."[1] This goes far to explain the necessity for drawing up contracts between donors and glass painters, and the stress laid in those contracts upon details, such as the proper painting, firing, and secure fixing of the glass, which nowadays would be taken for granted. A good example of one of these contracts was that drawn up in 1447 between the executors of the Earl of Warwick and John Prudde of Westminster, which is interesting enough to be quoted in full: "John Prudde, of Westminster, glasier 23 Junii 25 H. 6 covenanteth, etc., to glase all the windows in the new Chappell in Warwick with glasse beyond the seas, and with no glasse of England; and that in the finest wise, with the best, cleanest, and strongest glasse of beyond the seas that may be had in England, and of the finest colours; of blew, yellow, red, purpure, sanguine, and violet, and of all other colours that shall be most necessary to make rich and embellish the matters, images, and stories, that shall be delivered and appoynted by the said Executors by patterns in paper, after to be newly traced and pictured by another painter in rich colour, at the charges of the said glasier. All which proportions the said John Prudde must make perfectly to fine glase, eneylin it, and finely and strongly set it in lead and solder it as well as any glasse is in England. Of white glasse, green glasse, black glasse, he shall put in as little as shall be needful for the shewing and setting forth of the matters, images, and storyes. And the said glasier shall take charge of the same glasse wrought and to be brought to Warwick, and set it up there in

[1] This is the considered judgment of a distinguished antiquary. See Salzman's *Mediæval English Industries* (Oxford, 1923), p. 309.

the windows of the said Chapell; the Executors paying
to the said glasier for every foot of glasse 2s., and so
for the whole £91 1s. 10d."[1]

Again, the contract for the chapel windows of King's
College, Cambridge, drawn up in 1526 between the
College authorities and six London glass painters,
directed that the craftsmen "shalle at their owne
propre costes and charges, well, suerly, clenely, work-
manly, substantyally, curyously and sufficiently glase
and sette up . . . eightene wyndowes . . . with good,
clene, sure and perfyte glasse and oryent colors and
imagery of the story of the olde lawe and of the newe
lawe after the forme, maner, goodeness, curyousytie,
and clenelynes in every poynt of the glasse wyndowes
of the Kynge's newe chapell at Westmynster; and also
accordyngly and after such maner as oon Barnard
Fflower glasyer late deceased by Indenture stode bounde
to doo . . ."; also that they " shalle suerly bynde all the
seid wyndowes with double bands of leade for defence
of great wyndes and outrageous wetheringes. . . ."[2]

Nor was there any sentiment displayed by the
mediæval craftsman in charging for his work. A
donor got what he paid for, and nothing more, with
the result that the prices paid for finished windows
varied considerably, depending largely both upon the
designs and the individual firm employed. The rate
was nearly always reckoned, as indeed is the case
to-day, at so much per square foot. The highest price
recorded seems to have been the 2s. per foot (equal to
at least £1 of our money) paid in 1447 for the windows
of the Beauchamp Chapel in Warwick Church. Portions
of this glass which still survive in a much confused
condition (see Chapter X, Fig. 33) show that it was
of an exceptionally elaborate and ornate character,
which would explain the high price charged.

[1] Winston, *Memoirs Illustrative of the Art of Glass Painting* (London,
1865), p. 341; *Hints on Glass Painting* (2nd. ed., Oxford and London,
1867), i, p. 389.
[2] Winston, *Hints on Glass Painting*, vol. i, Appendix B, p. 390, note.

The windows of King's College Chapel, Cambridge, painted between 1515 and 1531 by a number of foreign glaziers, chiefly Flemings, and depicting for the most part Old and New Testament subjects (see Chapter XI, p. 129), cost between 1s. 4d. and 1s. 6d. the square foot, while most of the glass painted in 1442 by one John Glasier for the chapel of All Souls' College, Oxford, and depicting figures beneath canopies, cost its donor, Archbishop Chichele (who founded the college), 1s. per foot.[1]   Other prices recorded as paid for finished windows include £32 0s. 6d. paid in 1446–7 to John Prudde for " 640 feet of glass worked with divers pictures and borders " intended for windows at Eton College ; while 191 feet of " storied glass " (that is, subject windows) and 288 feet of glass " flourished with lilies and roses," and with certain arms, all intended for the hall windows of the same college, cost £23 3s. 4½d.[2] Or, to take one more example, " 1,336 feet of painted glass with borders of the King's arms " were purchased in 1351 from John Brampton and Henry Stathern at 13d. the foot, for sundry windows in Windsor Castle.[3]

---

[1] Ant. a Wood, *History of the Colleges and Halls in the University of Oxford* (ed. Gutch, 1786), p. 288, note.

[2] Willis and Clark, *Architectural History of the University of Cambridge*, vol. i. p. 394.

[3] Hope, *Windsor Castle*, vol. i, pp. 186, 206.

CHAPTER III

THE MEDIÆVAL GLASS PAINTERS

THERE seems to be a popular and widespread belief that the craftsmen who produced much of this glass painting were monks. In reality this was very far from being the case; indeed, with the exception of one, Theophilus, " a priest and monk " as he described himself, who in the twelfth century wrote a treatise on glass painting and other forms of fine art,[1] there is nothing to show that the monks knew anything at all about the subject.

It must be remembered that a monk was a man who retired from the world into a religious house in order to devote himself henceforth to the service of God. Such at least had been the high ideal set by the founders of monasticism; and though by the fifteenth century, when glass painting was most popular, many monastic establishments had fallen away considerably from these ideals, monks were still not allowed to mix freely with the outside world, nor were they in a position to study closely the frequent changes in costume and headgear, of which the glass painters showed such an intimate knowledge.

Moreover, generally speaking, the public were not allowed to enter any cathedral or church served by

---

[1] This work, the *Diversarum Artium Schedula* (i.e. a Treatise or Book about Various Arts), consists of three books, the first treating of painting, the second of the manufacture of glass, and the third of the working of metals, particularly with reference to the fabrication of sacred utensils. It was discovered about 1777 in the Ducal Library of Wolfenbüttel, and first published in its entirety in 1781. The section dealing with glass painting is reprinted with copious explanatory footnotes in Winston's *Hints on Glass Painting*, Appendix A.

a monastic order, unless it were a part set aside and screened off for parochial use, such as the naves of Wymondham Priory in Norfolk and Christ Church Priory in Hampshire, or unless the building in question contained the shrine or relics of some saint to which people in the town or strangers on pilgrimage would pay their devotions. Even then they were not allowed to wander where they chose, but were admitted at a certain door, conducted to the shrine or relics, allowed to pay their devotions and to make their contributions, and were then dismissed by the way whence they had come ; while the monastic buildings, other than the church, or those set apart for the lodging and entertainment of strangers and pilgrims, were all closed to the public.

But apart from this there is abundant evidence to show that the painted windows themselves reflected to the full the daily life and surroundings of the men who produced them (see Chapter V), while it must also be remembered that, long prior to the Reformation, the demand for painted glass was enormous and ever increasing, and that this beautiful form of decoration was as popular in secular buildings as it was in ecclesiastical (see Chapter XIV).

Who, then, were the mediæval glass painters ? The answer is simple. They were laymen, skilled craftsmen, who made the designing and production of painted glass their lifelong profession, just as is the case to-day. A lad began his apprenticeship in some glass-painter's shop, where he would be at the beck and call of everybody, receiving at the same time " the most perfect training in craftsmanship that can be given," namely, by " working with craftsmen and helping them with their work,"[1] and so gradually learning the craft by doing bits of it. He would probably begin by grinding the pigment used for shading and outline ; heating the soldering irons, melting solder, and other

[1] " The Picture Windows in New College Ante-Chapel," by Harry T. Powell, *Burlington Magazine*, viii (February 1906), p. 326.

simple tasks. From these he would gradually pass
on to the more elaborate work of making windows
by the processes described in Chapter II. He would
also be trained in design by the "master glazier"
himself, "by first piecing together figures, groups,
and heads from other cartoons, and adding new backgrounds, heads, and surroundings; then drawing
tracery, angels, and less important parts; until finally
he was able to draw a complete figure or composition."[1]

Much information respecting the olden-time glass
painters can be derived from such sources as municipal
records, fabric rolls, and contracts, as well as from
the wills of the men themselves, many of which have
been preserved. One or two extracts from these
sources may be quoted as further helping to refute
the idea that the monks painted the coloured glass
windows.

For example, about the middle of the fourteenth
century, Edward III began extensive building operations at Westminster Palace, including the erection of
a large chapel, where no expense was spared. In
1351 this chapel was ready to receive its coloured glass,
and in that year the King ordered writs to be issued
throughout Middlesex and twelve other counties com-
manding glass workers to assemble at Westminster.
They were to work at the glazing of the chapel windows
at the King's wages (which, it may be remarked, were
very liberal), and should there be any rebels or con-
trariants, they were to be detained until the King
should give order touching their punishment.[2] Yet,
a mere stone's throw from the Palace was the great
Benedictine monastery of St. Peter's, Westminster,
whence, had the monks been glass painters, sufficient
craftsmen could have been obtained with much less
trouble. Some particulars of the work carried out
by these men, and of their wages, have been given

---

[1] "Ancient Painted Glass," by J. A. Knowles, *The Builder*, May 19,
1922.

[2] J. T. Smith, *Antiquities of Westminster* (London, 1807), p. 83.

in Chapter II, pp. 10, 12, 13. Or, again, Sir John
Petty, glazier and Lord Mayor of York, bequeathed
in his will (1508) the sum of 13s. 4d. to Furness Abbey
" besechyng thame of clere absolution because I have
wroght mych work there."[1]

It should be pointed out that the title " glass painter "
was not used during the Middle Ages. The art was
introduced from France, and in consequence the early
craftsmen styled themselves or were styled " verrers "
or " verrours " (French *verre*), such as Robert le Verrer
of Colchester in 1295, or Walter le Verrour of York
in 1313. In the fourteenth century, however, when
there were probably as many Englishmen as Frenchmen
practising the art in this country, the title " verrour "
gradually gave place to that of " glasenwright " or
" glasswryghte," meaning a worker in glass, from the
Anglo-Saxon *wyrhta*, a worker, as the name by which
a glass painter should be styled, such as Thomas Glaswryghte of Gloucester, or John de Preston, Glasen-
wreght of York. By 1387 this title had in its turn given
place to the word " glasyer " or " glasier," which continued in general use until the seventeenth century,
when the term " glass painter " made its appearance.
It was used by John Aubrey, the Wiltshire topographer
and antiquary (1626–97), in speaking of " Old Harding
the glass painter of Blandford."[2] The expression
" glass stainer," used to denote a glass painter, was, as
already noted, an eighteenth-century invention first
used by William Peckitt of York (1731–95).

It is difficult to know how many glass painters were
at work at any given time in mediæval England, that
is, prior to the Reformation, when the art practically
ceased ; but there is good reason for believing that
the number was a large one. Mr. Wilfrid Drake has
collected the names of thirteen working in England
during the thirteenth century, seventy-five during the

[1] *Notes and Queries*, July 23, 1921 : " Glass Painters of York : Sir John
Petty," by J. A. Knowles.
[2] *Aubrey's Brief Lives*, ed. by A. Clark (Oxford, 1898), ii, p. 329.

fourteenth century, thirty-four in the fifteenth century, and thirty-three in the sixteenth century; the last-named including many Flemish and other foreigners to whom King Henry VII and his son Henry had granted letters of denization. Again, John Aubrey, who had probably obtained his information from " Old Harding the countrey glasse painter," whose workshops and furnaces he used to visit on play-days when at school at Blandford, says that " before the Reformation I believe there was no county or great town in England but had glasse painters."

In particular, York was a great centre of the art all through the Middle Ages, the Freemen's Roll of that city including the names of no less than 105 glaziers between 1313 and 1555, many of whom owned their own workshops and were not mere employees. " The work of the York glass painters was as well known on the west as on the east coast, and many churches and abbeys in the Lake District sent to York to have their windows painted."[1] London was, of course, another famous centre; Oxford seems to have been another; while it is perhaps worthy of remark that the ancient glass once filling the forty windows of Great Malvern Priory Church (glazed between 1440 and 1502), the remains of which are now collected into some sixteen windows,[2] proves upon careful examination to have been the work of at least ten distinct firms, only one of which can at present be definitely identified as existing elsewhere in England.[3]

It is a great mistake to imagine that these craftsmen were mere ignorant labourers, simply turning out windows by the hundred by what may seem to us very

[1] *Notes and Queries*, March 11 and 25, 1922: " Chronological List of York Glass Painters," by J. A. Knowles.

[2] Releaded between 1909 and 1917.

[3] The great east window of the choir, once containing twenty-four panels with Christ's Passion and Resurrection, besides the Twelve Apostles and other figures, bears every trace of being York work, probably that of John Chamber, junior, of that city, who died in 1450. See Mr. J. A. Knowles's article in the *Journal of the Society of Architects* for April 1922. The cover photograph and Fig. 10 reproduce two of the subjects.

mechanical and stereotyped methods. No doubt there were many little " jobbing " firms scattered up and down the country who could supply figures on simple quarry backgrounds (see Chapter X) to small parish churches at comparatively low prices, and whose style and technique were very poor. But the principals of some of the city and provincial firms were men of high standing and position, to be regarded and treated as such by those who employed them. Thus Thomas Glaswryghte of Gloucester, whose firm was in all probability responsible for the glazing of the great east window of Gloucester Cathedral (see Chapter IX, p. 97), was not only commissioned to work at the Royal Abbey of Westminster, but was further honoured by being invited to take part in a civic Commission of Inquiry.[1] Another eminent glass painter of his day was Thomas Glazier of Oxford, whose firm glazed the hall and chapel windows of William of Wykeham's great colleges at Oxford and Winchester[2] at the expense of their Founder. His kneeling portrait was actually inserted by way of a compliment in the east window of Winchester College chapel, glazed in 1393, and replaced by a modern copy in 1822. The copy shows the small figure of a man bearded but not tonsured, as would be the case if he were a member of any religious order. He is clad in the civilian dress of his day, a long gown, blue in this instance, with a maroon tippet. From his mouth issues a scroll lettered " Thōms opātor isti' vitri," for " Thomas operator istius vitri " (" Thomas the maker of this glass ").[3] It is evident that Thomas himself was a man of standing and position, since his portrait was allowed to be placed in a window of which, though the maker, he was not the donor ; while further evidence of his social standing is furnished

[1] *Transactions of the Bristol and Glos. Archæological Society*, vol. xl, pp. 147–66.

[2] New College, Oxford, founded in 1379, and Winchester College, founded in 1382, both by William of Wykeham, Bishop of Winchester from 1367 to 1404.

[3] Winston, *Memoirs*, p. 70 ; Nelson, *Ancient Painted Glass in England*, p. 40, Fig. 22.

by the hall-books of both colleges, which record that on several occasions he dined or supped at the high table on the dais in hall, a compliment not extended to everyone either in the Middle Ages or in the present day. Some of these men held high civic and other rank. A Winchester glass painter, one Henry Smart, represented that city in Parliament from 1455 to 1472. Sir John Petty, an eminent glass painter of York, took a prominent part in the municipal affairs of that city, holding in succession the offices of Chamberlain, Sheriff, Alderman, and finally Lord Mayor. He died in 1508 during his mayoralty, being buried with much ceremony " at the Parish Church of St. Michael called the Bel-frame [St. Michael le Belfrey] with the sword and mace borne by esquyers afore the body and corse, and six Aldermen—berying the sayd corse to the seyd church."[1]

In common with all pre-Reformation craftsmen, the glass painters were members of a Mystery or Craft Gild (Fig. 9).[2]   These gilds, which were the fore-runners of the present trade unions, were numerous wherever there were skilled artisans. " They were formed of men who followed the same occupation, and who united expressly for the protection of their trade, and to form regulations concerning their work, their apprentices, and servants, and the hours to be kept . . . and for a hundred matters which concerned themselves. . . . Each gild had its own governing officers, a Master and two or four Wardens ; in some companies assistants were added."[3]   The Gild of the London Glaziers was a powerful one. In 1474 they petitioned " The Right Honourable the Mair and the Aldermen of the Citee of London " against a number of foreign workmen who, not being members of their gild, were practising the art of glass painting in secret corners

---

[1] Notes and Queries, July 23, 1921 : " Glass painters of York : Sir John Petty," by J. A. Knowles, p. 64.

[2] J. A. Knowles, " The York School of Glass Painting," Journal Brit. Arch. Assoc., October 1923, p. 126 ; Architects' Journal, lviii (August 1923), p. 317.

[3] Mediæval England, edited by H. W. C. Davis (Oxford, 1924), p. 304.

and setting up their works (painted windows) in divers places in the city. They asked that this should be stopped and the offenders punished. Their petition was duly granted. Again, King Richard III forbade "painted glasses" (i.e. completed windows painted abroad) to be imported into England, no doubt with the idea of pleasing the Glaziers' Gild.

But with the accession of Henry VII in 1485 this happy state of affairs came to an abrupt termination, for both this monarch and his son King Henry VIII, who succeeded him in 1509, encouraged foreign crafts-men of all kinds, including glass painters, to come to England, " granting them letters of licence . . . dispensing them from the obligations imposed by the various restrictive statutes in nominal force,"[1] and employing them about the Royal courts in preference to English-men ; refusing at the same time to heed any petitions from the various craft gilds upon the subject. Barnard Flower, who held the responsible post of King's Glazier from 1505 until his death in 1517, was a foreigner, a " native of Almayn " (a German), while his successor, Galyon Hone, was also a foreigner, apparently a Fleming. These foreign glass painters, who lived for the most part in the parishes round about Southwark, were responsible, amongst other important works, for the glass in Henry VII's Chapel, King's College Chapel, Cambridge, and probably Fairford Parish Church (see Chapter XI).

Brief mention must be made of the official known as the King's Glazier. This office went back to early times, for one Edward is mentioned in 1242 as " chief glazier " at Windsor. Some ideas of the privileges attaching to the post may be obtained from the Patent Rolls for 1440, recording the appointment to that post of John Prudde. He was " to hold for life the office of glasyer of the King's works, to hold in such fees and

---

[1] *Mediæval England*, p. 590. See also the *Antiquaries Journal*, v. (1925), p. 148 : J. A. Knowles, " Disputes between English and Foreign Glass Painters in the Sixteenth Century."

wages as Roger Gloucester held by the hands of the
clerk of the works, and all other appurtenants, profits,
and a ' shedde called the glasyer logge ' in the western
part within Westminster Palace, and a gown of the
King's livery yearly at Christmas " ; while one of the
many saving clauses in the Act of Resumption, which
Parliament wrung from King Henry VI in 1450,
provided that nothing in the said Act should prejudice
John Prudde " oure glasyer " with regard to certain
grants of 12d. per day made to him by the King.[1]

The primary duties of the King's Glazier, who had
of course a staff of workmen under his direction, were
to undertake the glazing or repairing of windows in
the Royal Palaces and other residences, as well as those
in any building founded or erected by Royalty, such as
Eton College, founded in 1440 by King Henry VI,
where the coloured glass for the chapel and hall windows
was all painted by Prudde and his men,[2] or Henry
VII's Chapel, glazed between 1509 and 1515 by Barnard
Flower. A glimpse of his duties is given by an entry
in the Fabric Rolls of Windsor Castle for the year 1533,
where a payment of 8d. is recorded as made " to
Rychard Hyll of Wyndsore ffor hys horse to London
to fett Galyan the Kynges glasyer against the Kinge's
coming to Wyndsore." [3]

But the King's Glazier was also free to undertake
outside work as well. John Prudde, for instance,
glazed Fromond's Chantry in Winchester College with
coloured glass during 1443–4,[4] while the rich glazing
inserted in the Beauchamp Chapel at Warwick in 1447
(see Chapter X, p. 120) also came from his workshop.

---

[1] *Notes and Queries*, 12th Ser., iii (1917), p. 419 : " John Prudde, King's
Glasyer," by H. C.
[2] None of this glass now remains.
[3] Hope, *Windsor Castle*, vol. i, p. 250.
[4] Only a few fragments remain of this glass.

CHAPTER IV

RELIGIOUS LIFE OF THE MIDDLE AGES AND ITS INFLUENCE UPON CONTEMPORARY GLASS PAINTING

HOWEVER rough and uncivilised Mediæval England may seem to our present-day minds, it is abundantly clear that religion played a very much larger part in daily life than is the case to-day. This was especially the case with the fourteenth, fifteenth, and early sixteenth centuries. A Venetian traveller who visited this country at the beginning of the sixteenth century was struck by the way in which people attended to their religious duties. " They all attend Mass every day," he writes, " and say many Paternosters in public. The women carry long rosaries in their hands, and any who can read take the office of Our Lady with them, and with some companion recite it in church verse by verse after the manner of churchmen. On Sunday they always hear Mass in their parish church and give liberal alms. . . . Neither do they omit any form incumbent on good Christians." [1]

Apart from this, there are other evidences. Letters, for example, as well as legal documents, were very frequently dated by Saint's days, more rarely by the days of the month : " Monday next after St. Edmund the King," " St. Erkenwald," " St. Leonard's eve," and so forth. Pilgrimages were made by devout persons to various celebrated shrines both in England and on the Continent.

The miracle plays were another great attraction.

[1] Traill and Mann, *Social England* (1274–1509), vol. ii (London, 1903), p. 638.

These deserve more than a passing mention, for, as
will be seen, the glass painters derived many of their
ideas from them. They were usually performed upon
the Feast of Corpus Christi (Thursday after Trinity
Sunday), and were " run " by the Municipality ; while
the different trades and craft gilds, who were responsible
for their production, supplied the performers. The
plays were religious, being taken from the Old and
New Testaments, beginning with the Creation and
ending with the Last Judgment, but at the same time
containing a large comic element. They were acted
upon stages resembling huge cars, which could be
moved about as required, the whole of the action
taking place upon a single platform, beneath which
was a compartment used for a dressing-room, storing
properties, and the like. It is highly probable that
the comparative simplicity of the scenes in the pictorial
windows of the fourteenth and fifteenth centuries was
very largely inspired by the equally simple representations of Scriptural scenes in these miracle plays.

This religious zeal naturally manifested itself in
countless benefactions to the Church. Although, as
we have seen, people, generally speaking, were not
allowed to enter a monastic church unless a part of
it had been set aside for parish use, yet they frequently
contributed generously towards the foundation or
maintenance of the various monastic houses, receiving,
in return, the prayers of a particular community for
their welfare during life, and for the repose of their
souls after death. As the result of these benefactions,
the windows of monastic churches, with the possible
exception of those of the Cistercian Order (see Chapter
VI, p. 59), were usually filled with the richest painted
glass, much of it indeed being inserted at the cost of
secular donors, even of Royal rank. Thus the forty
windows of Great Malvern Priory Church were nearly
all glazed in this manner, Richard Duke of Gloucester
(afterwards Richard III) giving the great west window,
and King Henry VII the great window in the north

transept, while both the nave clerestories once commemorated various county families, including those of Besford and De Braci. Again, at Gloucester Cathedral (then a great Benedictine abbey) the enormous east window of the choir was glazed about 1350, at the cost of Thomas, Lord Bradeston, Constable of Gloucester Castle, as a memorial of the Battle of Crecy and of the following siege of Calais. The churches of the various orders of preaching or mendicant friars were adorned in precisely the same manner, the donors receiving in return the prayers of the fraternity.

It was usually the practice to insert kneeling figures of donors with their wives and families at the bottom of each window (see pp. 92–3, 106, 124). A direct allusion to this practice occurs in *The Creed of Piers the Plowman*, written at the end of the fourteenth century. In this poem, the author, an imitator of William Langland, lashes with merciless satire the various orders of friars. He represents himself as a poor man, ignorant of his Creed, to be instructed in the articles of which he applies in turn to the four orders of Mendicant Friars. All of them, he points out, seem to be unable to instruct him, but are ready enough to take money from him, the friar promising in return that—

> " Thou shouldest knely bifore Christ
> In compas of gold
> In the wide window west-ward
> Welnigh in the myddel
> And Saint Fraunceis hymselfe
> Shal folden the in his cope
> And present the to the Trinité
> And praye for thy synnes." [1]

The centre of all religious life in England was, however, the parish church. We can hardly realise to-day the appearance of an English parish church prior to the Reformation. Then the walls were bright with paintings of the saints and their lives and miracles. The

[1] Lines 245–52 in editions of *Piers Plowman* by T. Wright and by W. Skeat (Oxford, 1906). See also Winston, *Hints on Glass Painting*, i, Appendix D.

many altars with their reredoses were enriched with cunning craftsmanship and sculpture, and plentifully furnished with rich altar-cloths and hangings. There was a great store of copes, chasubles, and other vestments. The altar plate was of the finest quality that the gold and silver smiths could design and produce, even the poorest church being able to possess, so the above-named Venetian writer states, " crucifixes, candlesticks, censers, patens, and cups of silver." The rood-screens with their lofts that stretched across the chancel were not only richly carved but gorgeously painted and gilded, and their many panels decorated with repre-sentations of apostles, prophets, and saints. The many niches were filled with figures of saints, some-times of stone painted and gilded, or of alabaster, sometimes of silver, or even of gold. In East Anglia, the hammer-beam roofs, the pride of many a great church, were profusely enriched with carved angels who seemed to hover with outspread wings over the heads of the worshippers below. And, finally, the windows glowed and sparkled with brilliant coloured glass, setting forth Scriptural scenes or representations of the saints themselves in brave array.

All classes of society, high and low, vied one with another in giving money for the adornment and beautify-ing of their churches. It was, indeed, not uncommon, especially in the fifteenth century, for a rich merchant, say a wool-stapler or cloth-mercer, to erect a new church, or extensively repair and enlarge an older one, either at his sole cost or with the help of two or three friends. Thus at Fairford in Gloucestershire the little fourteenth-century church was pulled down about the year 1490, and the present splendid building erected at the sole cost of John Tame, a wealthy wool-merchant, who had come to live at Fairford,[1] his son Sir Edmund Tame completing the work by causing all the twenty-eight windows of the church to be filled with rich painted

[1] [John Leland, in his *Itinerary* (ed. Toulmin Smith, vol. i, p. 127), says that " Fairford never florishid afore the cumming of the Tames onto it."]

glass (see Chapters V and XI). Again, Stow, in his
Survey of London, says that one Sir John Hend, draper
and Mayor of London, was an especial benefactor to the
church of St. Swithun by London Stone, " as appeareth
by his arms in the glasse windows even in the tops of
them"[1]; while William Hampton, Mayor in 1472, caused
some of the windows of St. Christopher le Stocks[2] to
be glazed with coloured glass. The military classes,
barons, knights, and squires, alike were equally generous
in their gifts to the Church. " Old Sir Thomas Erping-
ham," who had commanded the archers at the Battle
of Agincourt in 1415, and whom Shakespeare has im-
mortalised as " a good old commander and a most
kind gentleman," gave the east window of the Austin
Friars' Church, Norwich, as a memorial to Norfolk
and Suffolk gentlemen who had died without male
issue[3] ; while another generous donor, Sir James
Tyrrell of Gipping in Suffolk, rebuilt and glazed part
of Gipping Church.[4]

The same generosity was equally marked among the
less wealthy classes. For example, the Churchwardens'
Accounts of Walberswick Church in Suffolk record
that in 1491 the sum of nine shillings was collected
" by a gaderyng of the wyves in the towne for a glas
wyndow "[5]; while St. Neot Church in Cornwall still
retains three windows given by the young men, the
young women, and the wives of the west side of the
parish respectively, a fourth window recording that
it was put up " at the gift and cost of Ralph Harris
and by his workmanship."[6] In many places people
formed themselves into gilds, agreeing to contribute

[1] Stow, *Survey of London* (Everyman's Library, Dent & Son, Ltd.),
p. 201.
[2] *Ibid.*, p. 167. The Bank of England covers the site of this church.
[3] Blomefield, *History of Norfolk*, vol. iv, pp. 86, 87.
[4] Nelson, *Ancient Painted Glass in England* (Methuen's Antiquary's
Books, 1913), p. 192.
[5] *Ibid.*, p. 42.
[6] J. P. Hedgeland, *Description of the Decorations to the Church of St.
Neot* (coloured plates, London, 1830); H. Grylls, *Descriptive Sketch of
the Windows of St. Neot Church*, 3rd ed. (Devonport, 1844).

certain fees to a common fund, to worship at a certain
church, and if necessary to keep that church in good
repair, or to maintain some of its altars. Bodmin
Church was rebuilt late in the fifteenth century by some
forty of these gilds " for the glory of God and the
good of man "; whilst the Lincolnshire churches of
Coningsby and Gosberton formerly possessed windows
set up in memory of the Brethren and Sisters of the
Gilds of Blessed Mary and of St. John Baptist respectively. The same lavish generosity was displayed
in countless mediæval wills, of which a single example
must suffice here, namely, that of Sir Robert Throckmorton, Lord of the Manor of Coughton [1] in Warwickshire, who in his will, dated 1518, bequeathed enough
money to fill the east window of Coughton Church with
the Story of the Doom (Last Judgment), and the
two windows at the east ends of the north and south
aisles with the Seven Sacraments and the Seven
Works of Mercy respectively. None of this glass is
in existence to-day.[2]

In erecting a painted glass window, whatever its
subject, it was usual to place an inscription at the foot,
setting forth the precise reason for its insertion and
often giving much valuable information concerning
the history of the church itself. Such inscriptions
were usually in Latin, but Norman-French was also
used, especially in the first half of the fourteenth century,
as at St. Mary's, Shrewsbury (see Chapter VIII, p. 88).
English, too, was used for this purpose, notably towards
the end of the fifteenth century and in the sixteenth,
as at Thornhill in Yorkshire (West Riding) and at St.
Neot, Cornwall.

As a rule these inscriptions, if in Latin, began :
" Orate pro " (pray for). If they went on " bono
statu " (good estate), or were simply worded " Orate
pro So-and-so," the person or persons referred to were

[1] Pronounced Coton.
[2] *Notices of the Churches of Warwickshire*, vol. ii (Warwick 1858), p. 139,
note (from Dugdale's *Antiquities of Warwickshire*).

still alive, and were in all probability the donors of the glass in question. But a legend beginning " Orate pro anima " or " animabus " (often written " a͞ıa " or " a͞ıabus " respectively) proved that the glass had been put up in memory of the persons concerned, as it now read " Pray for the *soul* [or souls] of . . ." A good example of an informative inscription was that formerly existing in a window of Mobberley Church, Cheshire,[1] which ran : " Orate pro anima Magistri Hamonis Leycestir rectoris hujus ecclesiæ qui hanc fenestram fieri fecit Anno Domini MCCCCLXXXXII " (" Pray for the soul of Master Hamon Leycester, rector of this church, who caused this window to be made in the year of our Lord 1492 "). It was evident, therefore, that the deceased rector had left enough money to glaze a window with coloured glass, and that his benefaction was acknowledged in the usual manner by a request for the repose of his soul. These invocatory inscriptions do not appear in post-Reformation glass.

Windows were sometimes put up to commemorate some notable event in national history or as war memorials. For example, the north transept window of Great Malvern Priory Church (which, however, was not used for parochial purposes) was glazed with rich coloured glass to commemorate the marriage of Arthur, Prince of Wales, with Catherine of Aragon, and still retains kneeling figures of that Prince, together with those of his father, Henry VII, and of two attendant knights. Since the inscription at the foot of the window asked for prayers for the " good estate " of the persons represented, the glass must have been put up during the Prince's brief married life, i.e. between November 1501 and April 1502, when he died of the plague at Ludlow Castle.

A war memorial window may still be seen in the Lancashire church of Middleton, put up by the parishioners to commemorate the great part played by a contingent of archers from that village at the

[1] Nelson, p. 62.

Battle of Flodden Field (fought September 11, 1513). The window in question contains figures of Sir Richard Assheton, the commander (who was knighted on the field as a reward for gallant conduct), his lady, the archers in jerkins blue, and their chaplain "Henry Taylyer," all kneeling in prayer. Each archer has his sheaf of cloth-yard arrows at his back, and his great war-bow, slung over his shoulder, and above him his name clearly inscribed upon a scroll.[1] Flodden was the last fight in which the longbow played any conspicuous part, and it is fitting that these English archers, who more than four centuries ago fought for their king and country, should yet remain kneeling in a window of the church where they once worshipped.

[1] From a *Guide to Middleton Church*; see also Nelson, p. 134.

CHAPTER V

SUBJECTS FOUND IN MEDIÆVAL PAINTED GLASS

It must be remembered that even by the sixteenth century education was by no means general, and that many people received the greater part of their religious instruction from the miracle plays or from the windows and walls of their parish churches. Hence the coloured windows served two distinct purposes, decoration and education. They formed, in fact, together with the almost equally common mural paintings, the picture-books of the Middle Ages, by which the clergy taught their congregations, fully realising that " that which the illiterate cannot comprehend from writing could be made plain to them by pictures." The mediæval glass painters drew their ideas and subjects from very many sources, some of which are almost unknown to us to-day, and had therefore a much greater field for the use and development of their imagination and skill. This was particularly the case during the fifteenth and early part of the sixteenth centuries, when men travelled more, and so gathered fresh ideas.

It is well to remember that the glazing of a great cathedral or abbey church would differ considerably in point of subjects from that of a small country parish church. Whereas the former would display pictorial representations of Scriptural incidents, saintly lives, and heraldic devices in its many windows, that of a parish church, unless erected by wealthy people, or attached (as many churches were) to some abbey, would consist of little more than figures set upon quarry fields, while the only thing in the nature of a " picture " window would probably be the simple Crucifixion group set in the east window of the chancel.

In studying mediæval windows it is always important to remember that the glass painter, in common with all mediæval craftsmen and designers (and for that matter many of post-mediæval date), was not an antiquary. He knew nothing of what we term " archæology," and but little of the customs and conditions prevailing in the East. In consequence, his daily life and surroundings were faithfully reflected in the works of art that he produced. Thus, in an Entry into Jerusalem, Christ would be represented as riding in at just such a gate as the artist would see at the end of his own High Street, the portcullis, the arrow-slits, and other features of defence against assault being all faithfully and accurately depicted (Cover).

Again, in representations of the Last Supper, Christ and His Disciples would be shown gathered round a table furnished with the same homely fare to which the artist himself would be accustomed. In Malvern Priory Church is a panel (Fig. 10) showing the Disciples seated on yellow benches round a table covered with a white cloth. One figure cuts a loaf of bread, another drinks from a chalice-like cup, whilst Christ Himself gives the sop, shown as a wafer, to Judas. The soldiers who arrest Christ as Judas gives Him the traitor's kiss, who guard Him as He stands before Pilate, or who sprawl in undignified attitudes of slumber as He steps forth from the Tomb, are life-studies from the knights and men-at-arms who clanked about the streets, the details of their armour changing, moreover, in accordance with the date of the glass, and being delineated with an accuracy impossible to men who had spent their lives in the seclusion of a cloister.

Or, to take one more example, there is in King's College Chapel, Cambridge (glazed between 1515 and 1531 by some of the Flemings resident in Southwark and adjacent parishes), a window, or rather two panels in a window, representing St. Paul's Farewell at Miletus.

In this scene is such a ship as the artist would see from his windows as she rode at anchor in the Pool of London—a three-masted craft with high poop and forecastle, and short deep waist. Her longboat lies alongside, whilst in the middle distance midway between ship and shore is the little cockboat sent in by the master to bring off St. Paul.

This ignorance of the customs and conditions of life in Palestine and the East sometimes led to the introduction of inaccurate and even absurd details. A notable example appears in a late fifteenth-century panel in the east window of St. Peter Mancroft Church, Norwich (Fig. 11), depicting the Adoration of the Infant Saviour by the Shepherds. " The Virgin sits on a bed nursing her new-born Child. On the bed there is a beautifully worked coverlet. At the foot of the bed is a Dutch brazier at which an attendant in a red robe and white veil is warming swaddling-clothes. . . . St. Joseph, wearing a pink robe with red hat, huddles in a quaint little arm-chair over the fire." It is evident that this artist " could only conceive of Christmastide in connection with the cold of an East Anglian climate"; and it is important to note that " precisely the same idea is expressed in the York mystery play of *The Journey to Bethelehem ; the Birth of Jesus*, where Joseph, standing outside the hut, is made to say :

> " A ! Lorde, what the wedir is colde !
> Ye fellest freese yat evere I felyd.
> I pray God helpe yam yat is alde,
> And namely yam yat is unwelde." [1]

Another example of ignorance, this time of geography, appears in a late fifteenth-century window of Gresford Church in Denbighshire, which illustrates the legendary story of Joachim and Anna (see p. 50). One panel depicts the Presentation of Mary in the Temple at Jerusalem (Fig. 12), and here a ship under sail is

[1] *The Fifteenth-century Glass in St. Peter Mancroft Church, Norwich*, by the Rev. Canon Meyrick (Goose & Son, Norwich), pp. 20, 21.

seen through an opening on the left, the designer of
this glass evidently imagining that Jerusalem was
situated on the coast.

It is also worthy of notice that in these ancient glass
paintings the artist relied almost entirely upon the
action of the various figures to denote emotion, and
not facial expression.   An exception to this rule was
usually made in windows depicting the Last Judgment,
which often exhibited a great variety of facial expression.

As already noted, both the mediæval glass painters
and their patrons had a very much larger choice of
subjects than is the case to-day.   They could fill their
windows with figures of saints, including not only the
Apostles, and such popular personages as Saints Nicholas,
Catherine, Margaret, or George, but hundreds of others,
whose very names are unknown to most of us to-day.[1]
These included royal, ecclesiastical, and monastic
saints, warriors, virgins, martyrs, hermits, and others,
one and all properly vested or armoured as befitted
their respective ranks, and usually represented as holding
their peculiar emblems, their names being inscribed
in Latin, especially after 1350, on the front of the bases
on which they stood.   It is important to remember
that in some cases the Latin form of a name differed
considerably from the English.   Examples are : " Jacobus " for James, " Hieronymus " for Jerome, " Holo-
fius " for Olaf, " Egidius " for Giles, " Leodegarius "
for Leger, " Eligius " for Eloi or " Loy," and " Sati-
vola " for St. Sidwell of Exeter.

The Nine Orders of Angels were often depicted in
glass, being usually placed in the traceries.   They are
divided into three distinct groups or hierarchies : first
Seraphim and Cherubim, adoring and praising, and
Thrones, who support the Throne of the Almighty.
The second group is that of the Governors who regulate
the Universe, and comprise Dominations, Virtues, and

---

[1] Messrs. Maurice and Wilfred Drake, in *Saints and their Emblems*
(London, 1916), collected the names of close upon 4,000 saints.

Powers; while the third order are the Messengers of God's Will, and consist of Principalities, Archangels, and Angels. Such was the latitude allowed to mediæval artists in depicting this subject that it seems almost impossible to find any two series treated alike.

Many saints were regarded both as patrons and as protectors, and for that reason were depicted again and again in windows, sometimes twice or three times in the same church. For example, St. Christopher, whose great popularity was due to the belief that anyone who had seen his image was for that day safe from sudden death, and for that reason was usually set as nearly opposite to the church door as possible, was represented no less than four times in the windows of Coxwold Church in the North Riding of Yorkshire. Again, St. Apollonia was invoked by those suffering from toothache : St. Lucy for diseases of the eye ; St. Margaret of Antioch by women in childbirth ; St. Roch against pestilence ; and Saints Agatha and Barbara against fire and lightning. Other saints were regarded as patrons and were venerated particularly upon that account. St. Catherine of Alexandria, for example, was the patron saint of schools, and of learning in general ; St. Leonard of prisoners and captives ; St. Nicholas of sailors, children, thieves, and pawnbrokers ; and St. Sitha or Zita of Lucca of house-keepers and servants.

It will be noticed that the Apostles when shown as a series were often represented, as at Drayton Beauchamp (Bucks) and Fairford (Glos), holding scrolls, each lettered with one clause of the Creed, which was tra-ditionally supposed to have been composed by the Twelve Apostles assembled in Council just before they separated for ever on their great work of evan-gelising the world. Under the prompting of the Holy Ghost each Apostle contributed one clause, so that the whole together formed a common rule and standard for the truth. This was the ancient Catholic faith, and its formula the all-accepted Apostles' Creed. In these representations the order in which the Apostles were arranged occasionally varied, St. James the Great changing places with St. John, the scroll of words unavoidably altering with the position. The usual order was as follows, the inscriptions being frequently contracted, especially when space was limited.

1. St. Peter, with his keys of gold and silver. "Credo in Deum Patrem Omnipotentem creatorem coeli et terræ" ("I believe in God the Father Almighty, Maker of heaven and earth").

2. St. Andrew, with a saltire or **X**-shaped cross. "Et in Iesum Christum Filium ejus unicum Dominum nostrum" ("And in Jesus Christ His only Son our Lord").

3. St. James the Greater, frequently wearing a pilgrim's "slavyn" or rough hairy garment, with scallop-shell and staff. "Qui conceptus est de Spiritu Sancto, natus ex Maria Virgine" ("Who was conceived by the Holy Ghost, Born of the Virgin Mary").

4. St. John, usually holding a chalice with a dragon emerging therefrom.[1] "Passus est sub Pontio Pilato, crucifixus, mortuus, et sepultus" ("Suffered under Pontius Pilate, Was crucified, dead, and buried").

5. St. Thomas, with spear. "Descendit ad inferna, tertia die resurrexit a mortuis" ("He descended into hell; The third day He rose again from the dead").

6. St. James the Less, with a fuller's club. "Ascendit ad coelos, sedit ad dexteram Dei Patris omnipotentis" ("He ascended into heaven, And sitteth on the right hand of God the Father Almighty").

7. St. Philip, with a foliated cross or three loaves. "Inde venturus est judicare vivos et mortuos" ("From thence he shall come to judge the quick and the dead").

8. St. Bartholomew, with knife. "Credo in Spiritum Sanctum" ("I believe in the Holy Ghost").

---

[1] This refers to the legend that the saint was challenged by a priest of Diana to drink a draught of poison, and that upon making the sign of the cross over the cup, Satan rose from it in the form of a dragon and flew away.

9. St. Matthias, usually with a halberd. " Sanctam Ecclesiam Catholicam, sanctorum communionem " (" The holy Catholic Church ; The Communion of Saints ").

10. St. Simon with a saw (the emblem of his martyrdom), fish, or boat. " Remissionem peccatorum " (" The Forgiveness of sins ").

11. St. Jude, with boat or a club. " Carnis resurrectionem " (" The Resurrection of the body ").

12. St. Matthew, various emblems. " Et vitam eternam. Amen " (" And the life everlasting. Amen ").

Perfect series of Apostles with Creed-scrolls remain at Fairford (Glos) and at Gresford in Denbighshire, both late mediæval in date ; while there are complete seventeenth-century series at Wadham College and at Lincoln College, Oxford. Imperfect series remain in many churches, notably at Drayton Beauchamp (Bucks), Hamstall Ridware (Staffs), Coughton (Warwicks), Nettlestead (Kent), and in the great west window of Winchester Cathedral.

It was also the practice to set up windows containing the Twelve Prophets, each with a scroll bearing some passage from the Old Testament, intended as a parallel to the corresponding Creed clause, as at Fairford, and formerly in the great west window of Winchester Cathedral. These prophets were never nimbed, neither did they carry emblems.

Their usual order, corresponding to that of the Apostles in the list just given, was as follows :

1. Jeremias. " Patrem invocabitis qui fecit et condidit coelos " (" You shall call Me Father, Who made and built the heavens ").

2. David. " Deus dixit, en Filius meus es tu ; ego hodie genui te " (" The Lord said to me, Behold, thou art My son, to-day have I begotten thee ").

3. Isaias. " Ecce virgo concipiet et pariet filium " (" Behold, a virgin shall conceive, and bear a son").

4. Zacharias. " Suscitabo filios tuos " (" I will raise up thy sons ").

5. Oseas (Hosea). "O mors, ero mors tua; ero morsus tuus, O inferne" ("O death, I will be thy destruction; O hell, I will be thy sting").

6. Amos. "Qui edificat in coelum ascensionem" ("He that buildeth an ascent to heaven").

7. Sophonias (Zephaniah). "Et accedam ad vos in judicio et ero testis velox" ("And I will come to you in judgment, and I will be a speedy witness").

8. Joel. "In valle Josaphat judicabit omnes gentes" ("In the valley of Jehoshaphat He shall judge all nations").

9. Micheas (Micah). "Invocabuntur omnes eum et servient ei" ("All shall call upon Him, and they shall serve Him").

10. Malachias. "Cum odium habueris dimitte" ("When thou shalt hate her, put her away").

11. Daniel. "Educam vos de sepulchris vestris, popule meus" ("I will lead you out of your sepulchres, O My people").

12. Abdias (Obadiah). "Et erit regnum Domini. Amen" ("And the Kingdom shall be the Lord's. Amen").

A complete series remains at Fairford in Gloucestershire (see H. W. Taunt's Guide to the church), and remains of others at New College, Oxford, and King's College Chapel, Cambridge, in Brassie's Chantry.

It should here be noted that the rich vestments, especially those depicted as worn by royal and ecclesiastical saints, were official or conventional, and not articles of everyday wear in the Middle Ages. The cope, for instance, which was a semi-circular mantle of very rich design worn by ecclesiastics, was chiefly a processional vestment (see Fig. 38). Again, the chasuble and dalmatic over the white alb, which episcopal saints were usually shown as wearing (see Fig. 30), or the dalmatic over alb worn by deacons such as St. Stephen, were used only at the Mass. Benedictine saints, such as St. Benedict or St. Maurus, were usually depicted, especially after the middle of the fourteenth century, as wearing deep blue, owing to the difficulty of reproducing black (the proper colour of their habit) in painted glass.

Picture windows were equally popular, their subjects being drawn from a large variety of sources. The picture Bibles and other works of a like kind, such as the *Speculum Humanæ Salvationis* (or *Mirror of Man's Salvation*), were favourite sources of inspiration. These works were produced in MS., chiefly by secular labour, and contained scenes from the Old and New Testaments. The *Speculum Humanæ Salvationis* contained two pictures only on each page, one from the Old and one from the New Testament, set side by side, with two columns of text below. The *Biblia Pauperum* differed from this in having three pictures on a page, the central subject being taken from the New Testament, the side ones from the Old, with, in addition, half-figures of prophets connected with the framework round them, the text being fitted within the architecture or upon scrolls held by the figures, the whole forming an elaborate commentary upon the life of Christ. Remains of two series of windows based directly upon these pictorial commentaries still exist in English glass : one of twelfth-century date in Canterbury Cathedral (see Chapter VI, p. 60) ; the other of early sixteenth-century date in King's College Chapel, Cambridge (Chapter XI, pp. 129, 134). A third series of late fifteenth-century date set up by Cardinal Morton, Archbishop of Canterbury (1486–1500), in Lambeth Palace Chapel, perished in the Civil War.[1]

Both the Old and the New Testaments were, of course, freely drawn upon as window subjects, especially during the fourteenth and fifteenth centuries. Thus, in York Minster, the upper half of the great east window was filled with a series of twenty-seven panels, each about a yard square, from Old Testament history, beginning with God creating the world and ending with the death of Absalom ; while the lower half contained eighty-one panels illustrating the Revelation of St.

[1] See Winston, *Hints on Glass Painting*, vol. i, p. 407 note.

John.   The firm employed was that of John Thornton
of Coventry.   Again, the south nave clerestory of Great
Malvern Priory formerly contained seventy-two panels
(twelve in each of six windows) with Old Testament
scenes[1]; while Durham Cathedral formerly possessed
" a goodly faire great glasse window called Joseph's
window, the which hath in it all the whole storye of
Joseph most artificially wrought in pictures in fine
coloured glass accordinge as it is sett forth in the Bible,
verye good and godly to the beholders thereof."[2]

The Malvern Old Testament windows mentioned
above seem to have been a particularly interesting
and elaborate series.   Each of six tall windows contained twelve panels arranged in four rows of three
pictures apiece, their fields counter-changing red with
blue.   The first window began with the Creation,
and agreed closely with other contemporary series.
The Almighty plans the world with a pair of com-
passes ; creates sun, moon, and stars, birds and fishes,
animals, and finally man.   Adam and Eve are placed
in the Garden of Eden, shown as surrounded by a city
wall with towers ; they are tempted by the serpent,
whose human head, as usual in mediæval art, wears a
fashionable lady's head-dress ; they are detected and
expelled, and so forth.   The other windows dealt with
the lives of Noah, Abraham, Jacob, Joseph, Moses, and
Aaron.   Portions of all these remain and contain many
interesting details, one of which, though not actually
taken from Scripture, may be mentioned here.   The
story of the Israelites worshipping the golden calf
(as given in Exod. xxxii.) relates that the idol was
ground to powder and mixed with water, and that
the worshippers were made to drink the mixture.   But
Jewish tradition adds that when this had been done,
the guilty persons turned yellow, thus making their

---

[1] Thirty-three of these panels are now in the three windows of the
south choir aisle, fragments of several more being scattered throughout
various other windows.

[2] *Rites of Durham* (Surtees Society), p. 3.

detection an easy matter. One panel illustrates this
scene. A group of men, of whom two have yellow
beards, drink the mixture from bowls, Moses standing
by ; while in the foreground a man with yellow hair
and beard is about to be beheaded by a burly swords-
man clad in red.

Other Old Testament series or fragments thereof
remain at :

St. Neot, Cornwall. The Creation, etc., in fifteen
panels, and the Deluge in eight, Noah's ark being shown
as a three-masted ship.[1]

Barkway, Herts. A panel with the Creation of
Trees and Plants.[2]

Thaxted, Essex. Three panels from a Creation
window : (1) Adam and Eve in the Garden ; (2) Eve
eating the Forbidden Fruit ; (3) The Expulsion.[3]

Hereford Cathedral. A window over the door leading
into the cloisters has some fragments of a history of
Joseph.

Lincoln Minster has a number of thirteenth-century
panels with Old Testament subjects, but it is not clear
whether they once formed part of a *Biblia Pauperum*
set, or whether they came from an Old Testament
series. The former is the more probable.

The New Testament series usually depicted the life
of Christ, as at East Harling and St. Peter Mancroft
Church, Norwich, both of fifteenth-century date and
by the same makers [4] ; at St. Kew in Cornwall, and
formerly in the north nave aisle of Great Malvern
Priory (where twelve panels remain out of sixty) ;
but scenes from the Acts of the Apostles fill two windows
at King's College Chapel, Cambridge, while the whole
of the lower half of the great east window of York
Minster was filled between 1405 and 1408 with the
story of the Revelation of St. John.

---

[1] Nelson's *Ancient Painted Glass in England*, p. 63.
[2] *Ibid.*, p. 100.
[3] *Ibid.*, p. 85.
[4] Meyrick, op. cit., pp. 61–5.

It should be remembered that the Bible of the Middle Ages, whence all these Scriptural incidents were taken, was not the present-day Authorised Version, but that known as the Vulgate (Editio Vulgata ; *vulgata* = popular), which was the Latin translation made by St. Jerome from the Hebrew of the Old Testament, and the Greek of the New, during the years A.D. 383–405. For over a thousand years it was the sole form in which the Bible was known to Western Europe, and it remains to-day the Authorised Version of the Roman Catholic Church.

The various apocryphal gospels, such as the Prot-evangelium of James, the Gospel of the Pseudo Matthew, together with other writings of a like kind, were also drawn upon for window subjects. These works began to be produced, so far as is known, as early as the second century, which, indeed, seems to have been a perfect hot-bed for the production of writings of this type. With few exceptions, these apocryphal gospels were repudiated and condemned by the Church, and only later and in a modified form did their stories pass into the general Catholic tradition.

It was the practice in the Middle Ages to preface the Life of Christ with a series of pictures of the Birth and Upbringing of Mary, beginning with the story of Joachim and Anne, the grandparents of Jesus, as related in the Prot-evangelium of James. Sometimes the story was told in three or four panels only, as at Fairford and King's College Chapel, Cambridge ; sometimes it was made to fill an entire window, as at Great Malvern, where the first window of the above-named New Testament series was entirely devoted to the story of Joachim and Anne, the parents of the Virgin. The story is interesting enough to be related in brief. Joachim and Anne were good and prosperous people, but old and childless. Because they were childless, the High Priest refused their offering in the Temple, whereupon Joachim retired in sadness to the country. An angel appeared, first to his wife, Anne, who had

remained in Jerusalem, and then to Joachim, bidding
them both to meet at the golden gate of the Temple,
and promising that a daughter should be born to them
who should be blessed by all generations. In due time
the child was born and was named Mary. At the age
of three she was taken to the Temple, where she walked
up the fifteen steps of the altar of her own accord.
Thenceforth she lived in the Temple, being fed and
ministered to by angels. When Mary grew up, the
High Priest was bidden by an angel to summon all the
unmarried men in Israel in order that a husband might
be chosen for her. Each man was instructed to bring
a rod with him, and he in whose rod a sign was seen
should be selected. Joseph, though an old man, had
to come with the rest, and his rod budded and burst
into leaf and flower, while a dove flew out of it and
perched upon his head.

The Lives of the Saints with their miracles and
martyrdoms were equally popular as subjects, but,
like the Scriptural windows, were not of common
occurrence in small parish churches. Most of these
saintly Lives were taken from the work known as the
Legenda Aurea, or *Golden Legend*. This was a series
of stories collected by Jacobus de Voragine (about
1230–98), a friar of the Order of St. Dominic, who
subsequently became Archbishop of Genoa. The name
given to this collection by its author was simply *Legends
of the Saints*, but it came to be known as the *Golden
Legend*, for, as Wynkyn de Worde said, " Like as
passeth gold in value all other metals, so this Legend
exceedeth all other books." It was translated into
French from the original Latin by Jean de Vigny in
the fourteenth century, and was produced by Caxton
in English in 1483. It formed the great storehouse of
legendary lore in the Middle Ages.[1]

Other mediæval collections of saintly miracles were

[1] Westlake, *Parish Gilds of Mediæval England*, p. 126. Caxton's version
of the *Golden Legend* has been published by Messrs. Dent in their Temple
Classics (7 vols.).

the *Dialogus Miraculorum,* or *Dialogue of Miracles,*
compiled by Cæsarius of Heisterbach, who died in
1240, and the *Speculum Historiale,* or *Mirror of History,*
by Vincent of Beauvais (died 1264). In addition to
these there were numerous miracles and legends of
saints which were well known in the Middle Ages, but
of which no modern record seems to exist.

Among windows of this kind still remaining in England
may be mentioned the Life of St. Laurence in the east
window of Ludlow Church, Shropshire; of St. Cuthbert
of Durham and St. William of York in York Minster;
of St. Helen at Ashton-under-Lyne Church in Lancashire; and of St. Catherine in York Minster, Balliol
College, Oxford, Clavering Church in Essex, and Combs
Church in Suffolk, portions only remaining of the last
three examples. Windows depicting the lives of more
or less local saints still exist in Morley Church, Derbyshire, where are seven panels from a Life of St. Robert
of Knaresborough (removed with much more glass
from Dale Abbey in the same county), and at St. Neot
Church, Cornwall, where a window illustrates the life
of that little-known saint.

A very favourite window subject, especially in the
fourteenth century, was the design known as the Tree
of Jesse. This was really a pictorial genealogical table
illustrating our Saviour's maternal descent from Jesse,
the father of King David. The idea was evidently
based upon Acts xiii. 22, 23. The general scheme was
broadly always the same, the details differing with the
various periods of glass painting. Jesse himself either
lay, sat, or crouched at the foot of the window, and
from him rose a great vine-stem spreading outwards
and upwards through the lights and bearing coloured
leaves and bunches of fruit. The stem was twisted
into graceful loops and ovals, wherein stood or sat the
various kingly descendants of Jesse, richly clad and
holding swords or sceptres, while the outermost lights
usually contained the figures of the prophets who foretold the coming of Christ. The series terminated with

the Virgin Mary holding the infant Saviour in her arms. Good examples of Jesse windows remain at Wells Cathedral, Ludlow, Selby Abbey, and Shrewsbury (St. Mary's Church), all of the fourteenth century; Margaretting, Essex, and Leverington, Cambridge, of the fifteenth century; and Dyserth and Llanrhaiadr in Wales, of the sixteenth century.

Occasionally windows were put up to illustrate the works of some popular theological writer. A good example of this type still remains in All Saints' Church, North Street, York. It illustrates the Fifteen Signs of the End of the World, as foretold in a poem, *The Pricke of Conscience*, written in Northumbrian dialect by one Richard Rolle of Hampole, " the remarkable product of a remarkable age. He was born about 1290 at Thornton in Yorkshire, and after studying at Oxford devoted himself to the contemplative life and lived as a recluse till his death in 1349. His sanctity was so great that there was an expectation of his canonisation, which, however, was not realised. The output of his devotional writings during his long retirement was immense. He translated portions of the Bible into English many years before Wycliffe, and the popularity of his works is sufficiently attested by the large number of MSS. in the British Museum, Bodleian, and other libraries. His chief work, *The Pricke of Conscience*, which inspired this window, was written in Northumbrian dialect, and treated of the beginning of man's life, death, and why death is to be dreaded, purgatory, doomsday, and the pains of hell and joys of heaven. . . ." The window illustrates that part dealing with the last fifteen days of the world, as related by St. Jerome, "who in turn, no doubt, derived his inspiration from the Book of Revelation." The pictures, which start at the left-hand bottom corner and follow to the right, include an extraordinary inundation of the sea, followed by its subsiding; fishes and sea-monsters coming on to the land and making a great noise; the sea and trees on fire; earthquakes; men

hiding in holes in the earth; the stars falling from
heaven; death and mourning; and finally the end of
all things. Each panel has an explanatory legend
beneath in Northumbrian dialect, and in effect a brief
paraphrase of the corresponding verse in the poem
itself. Thus, for example, the event for the fifth day,
namely, the Sea on Fire, is explained by :

> " Ye fift day ye sea sall bryn
> And all ye waters that may ryn "—

whereas the poem itself reads :

> " Ye fift day ye se sal brynne
> And alle waters als yai sal rynne ;
> And yat sal last fra ye son rysyng
> Til ye tyme of ye son down gangyng." [1]

Another example of a window illustration of the
works of a popular theological writer occurs at Greystoke
Church, Cumberland, where are a number of panels
of early sixteenth-century date depicting the adven-
tures of the Apostles Matthew and Thomas at the
City of Wrondon, as related by one Leucius Charinus,
whose works were declared heretical by Pope Gelasius
in the fifth century.[2]

Other subjects frequently set up in glass were the
Seven Sacraments : Baptism (by total immersion),
Confirmation (of children in arms, or even in swaddling
bands), Marriage, Penance, Holy Orders, Holy Communion (usually illustrated by the consecration of
the Host in the Mass), and Extreme Unction (or
administration of the last Rites to the Dying). These
were all grouped about a central figure of Christ,
either risen or crucified, from Whose Wounds streams
of blood flowed into each Sacrament. In five of these
Sacraments the officiating minister was usually a
priest ; the others, Confirmation and Ordination, re-
quiring the presence of a bishop. In one or two cases

---

[1] Shaw, *An Old York Church, All Saints', North Street, York*, p. 33.

[2] Nelson, *Ancient Painted Glass in England*, p. 67, where the story
is given in full.

each rite was performed by a bishop, as at Buckland Church (Glos) (where three panels from a series remain), or even by an archbishop, as at Great Malvern.

No perfect window seems to have been preserved, but at Crudwell (Wilts) five Sacraments are grouped around a figure of the Risen Christ; while at Doddiscombleigh Church in Devonshire is a partially restored window with all seven, but with a new central Christ. Other less perfect examples, consisting for the most part of two or three panels only, remain at Buckland (Glos), Cartmel Fell (Lancs), Combs (Suffolk), Durham Cathedral, Great Malvern Priory (Worcs), Melbury-Bubb (Dorset), and Tattershall Church (Lincs).

The Seven Deadly Sins—Anger, Avarice, Envy, Gluttony, Lust, Pride, and Sloth—remain only at Newark-upon-Trent, and this series in fragments, including Gluttony as a man with a bowl in his hand and a jug slung on his belt. Another popular window subject was the Seven Works of Mercy: Feeding the Hungry, Giving Drink to the Thirsty, Clothing the Naked, Housing the Stranger, Visiting the Sick, Visiting the Prisoners, and Burying the Dead. These remain in All Saints', North Street, York (excepting the last named), and Messing, Essex (seventeenth-century enamel glass); while there are portions of sets at Chinnor (Oxon) (fourteenth century), Combs (Suffolk), and Tattershall (Lincs).

The Te Deum was another subject found in ancient glass, and, like the Nine Orders of Angels, provided much scope for the imagination of the designer. No perfect example remains, but there are important portions of windows at York Minister (in west aisle of south transept), Hope Church in Flint, and Morley Church, Derbyshire. The Magnificat and Nunc Dimittis treated pictorially remain, although, alas! only in á fragmentary condition, in the north transept of Great Malvern Priory Church.

Among other remarkable window subjects may be mentioned the Story of the Holy Cross at Morley,

Derbyshire, and the Dance of Death in St. Andrew's
Church, Norwich.   The latter subject, now only represented by a single panel, which depicts a skeleton
leading by the hand a bishop in full vestments, formerly
showed Death dancing off with people of all ages,
degrees, and conditions. This grisly subject (which
once decorated the cloister walls of the " Pardon
Churchyard " of Old St. Paul's) seems to have been
inspired by the frightful mortality caused by the Black
Death in 1349–50.

Mention should be made of a most remarkable
window formerly existing at Heydon Church, Norfolk,
which represented the pains inflicted by the sins of
man upon the Redeemer. In the centre was the
Crucified Christ, while round about Him were twelve
young dicers, drinkers, blasphemers, and other evil-
doers, each with an inscribed scroll issuing from his
mouth. The curious inscriptions in English are recorded by Blomefield.[1] All traces of this remarkable
window have long since vanished.

The Doom or Last Judgment was a favourite window
subject in the Middle Ages, although comparatively
few examples have survived until the present day.
It was of course intended to remind worshippers of
the terrors consequent upon sinful deeds, and of the
wonders and horrors of Eternity, and for that reason
was usually realistic in the extreme. Its actual situation in the church varied according to individual circumstances, but was always a prominent one, usually
the great east or great west window. It also occurred
in the traceries of Jesse windows, as at Wells Cathedral
(circ. 1340), Selby Abbey, and at Winchester College
Chapel, the last named replaced in 1822 by a modern
copy (see Chapter XIII, p. 149). The general arrangement was always the same, the details varying according
to the space at the artist's disposal, and also according
to his powers of imagination. In the centre or perhaps
at the top was Christ seated in Majesty upon the Rain-

[1] Blomefield, *History of Norfolk*, vol. vi, p. 253

bow, and displaying His Wounds; the Virgin Mary and St. John the Baptist being usually placed one on each side in act of intercession. The Apostles were sometimes present, as at Tewkesbury Abbey, an early example of the subject, and at Fairford; while the traceries were usually filled with angels blowing trumpets to summon the dead to judgment or holding Passion emblems.

In the lower part of the window were figures rising from their graves, St. Michael with the scales being shown also (e.g. at Fairford). The saved pass into heaven, being met at the gate by St. Peter with his keys, while the lost were depicted as being dragged, carried, or carted off to hell, represented as a huge dragon-mouth belching out flames. A notable feature of all these Doom windows was that some of the risen dead, both saved and lost, were depicted as wearing papal tiaras, mitres, or crowns, the idea being to show that no person, whatever his rank might be in this world, could hope to escape punishment for his evil deeds in the next. In the Winchester College Judgment, kings and bishops were included among both saved and lost; while at Ticehurst in Sussex (where are important fragments of a fine mid-fifteenth-century Doom window) two of the lost wear a tiara and a crown respectively. Again, a window formerly at Tattershall in Lincolnshire (see Chapter XV, p. 163), representing Hell's Torments, included " divers Creatures bound togeather in a chayne; amongst whom one with a Crowne, another with a Mytre on his head, ye Divell tormenting them."[1] Of the punishments shown as being inflicted upon the lost in these Doom windows, it is sufficient to say that they reflect all too faithfully mediæval beliefs and imaginations.

[1] Gervase Holles, "Lincolnshire Church Notes" (*Lincoln Record Society*, vol. i), p. 141.

CHAPTER VI

NORMAN OR TWELFTH-CENTURY GLASS
(1170–1200)

As far as England is concerned, the earliest mention of glass in connection with church windows appears to be A.D. 680, when Benedict Biscop, Abbot of Wearmouth, sent over to France for glaziers to work in his newly erected stone churches of Jarrow and Wearmouth, while a few years later, in A.D. 709 to be precise, St. Wilfrid caused the windows of York Minster (the predecessor of the church which, begun in the eleventh century, was not finished till the fifteenth) to be glazed also. What sort of glass was actually used by these early craftsmen is not definitely known, but as coloured glass windows were known on the Continent in very early times, as early indeed as the days of Chrysostom and Jerome (circ. 410), it is at least possible that these first English church windows consisted of something more than white glass; probably pieces of coloured unpainted glass, arranged in crude attempts at patterns, which were outlined and held together with leadwork.

It is difficult, indeed, to know the origin *of painted glass windows*, for the numerous references to the subject of coloured windows made by early Continental writers and eyewitnesses all clearly refer to unpainted glass—that is, glass coloured in its manufacture, but devoid of any picture or pattern made by the application of vitrifiable pigment. But after the introduction into Western Europe of the art of enamelling towards the end of the tenth century, namely, about A.D. 972, we begin to read of painted glass windows; while by the beginning of the eleventh century such progress

58

had been made in the art that a treatise on the subject, the famous *Diversarum Artium Schedula* (or *A Book about Various Arts*) was compiled by a monk named Theophilus (see Chapter III), which clearly explained the whole process of designing and making a painted glass window as then understood, a process not differing very greatly from the methods in vogue to-day. It is probable that the oldest glass now in existence, namely, the five figures of Prophets (Moses, David, Daniel, Hosea, and Jonah), which remain in the cathedral of Augsburg, was painted about the middle of the eleventh century. These, as a German writer points out, are obviously the results of a fully developed style, not a first attempt.[1]

From this time onwards until a century or so after the Norman Conquest no further mention is made of glass in connection with English churches, although the art was making great strides on the Continent, so much so that in 1134 the Cistercian Order was forbidden to use other than white glass in the windows of their churches, an austerity which was considerably modified by the fifteenth century, as fragments of coloured glass have often been dug up during excavations on the sites or ruins of Cistercian monasteries. But late in the twelfth century, apparently about 1170, when things had settled down somewhat after the Norman Conquest, French glass painters began to come over to England to glaze the great cathedral churches newly erected by the Normans.

Eminent authorities are agreed that there was a great centre of glass painting at Chartres about that time, and it is certain that much of the twelfth-century glass in England agrees very closely in technique and general detail with the contemporary work still remaining in Chartres Cathedral, as also with that in windows at Sens, and with that formerly in Rheims Cathedral,

---

[1] J. L. Fischer, *Handbuch der Glasmalerei* (Leipzig, 1914), p. 45. I am indebted to Mr. G. McN. Rushforth, F.S.A., for calling my attention to this reference. See also Lewis Day's *Windows.*

alas ! mostly destroyed by German shell-fire during the Great War.[1] Very little twelfth-century glass still exists in this country to-day, for three distinct reasons :

(1) The earliest known date of glass painters working here after the Conquest was not before 1170 ; consequently there was not time to do a very great quantity of work.

(2) By reason of the labour involved in grozing out and shaping the large number of small pieces which made up the panels, glass of this period must have been exceedingly costly, and was therefore probably only placed in a few churches.

(3) Of the glass actually executed during this period, much was destroyed by subsequent rebuildings and consequent re-glazings of the churches in which it was placed. An example of this destruction by rebuilding occurred at York when the great twelfth-century choir erected in the time of Archbishop Roger (1154–1181) was pulled down and entirely rebuilt between 1361 and 1423, being glazed afresh in the styles then prevalent, with the result that only a few scattered panels of the earlier glazing were saved and leaded into various clerestory windows of the nave.

Of the twelfth-century glass still existing in this country, by far the greatest portion is to be found in Canterbury Cathedral (where it was placed about the year 1184), although for the most part no longer actually *in situ*. It originally consisted of twelve medallion windows containing New Testament subjects, each with their respective Old Testament types taken, as already explained, from the *Biblia Pauperum* (see page 47). Of these twelve windows, three only remain, two having been patched up with remains of several others[2] ;   the third, which represents the Crucifixion, Entombment, Resurrection, Ascension, and Pentecost, each surrounded by *four* Old Testament types, has been extensively restored, and contains a

---

[1] Landrieux, *The Cathedral of Reims* (London, 1920), p. 122.
[2] For the subjects represented, see Nelson, p. 104.

large proportion of new glass. There were also forty-two clerestory windows filled with the Ancestry of Christ, beginning with the Almighty and Adam, and terminating with the Virgin Mary and our Lord : eighty-four figures in all. Of this wonderful series, no less than thirty-eight figures still remain (see below, Fig. 14), although no longer *in situ*, having been for the most part transferred in 1799 to the great perpendicular windows of the south transept and nave (see page 165).

Smaller quantities of twelfth-century glass still exist in various windows of York Minster, also in Dorchester Abbey in Oxfordshire, and in Brabourne Church in Kent. Some panels of this date in Rivenhall Church, Essex, brought from Chenu-sur-Sarthe (Maine-et-Loire) in France,[1] also some French medallions in Wilton Church near Salisbury, may be mentioned for purposes of study.

It is important to remember at this point that though each period of mediæval glass painting, both English and Continental, has its own peculiar characteristics, not to be found in any other style, yet the work produced by individual glass painters is naturally apt to vary considerably both in technique and in detail, so that the work at Canterbury differs from that at York, and that at Dorchester (Oxon) from either.

All glass of this first period was divided into five distinct types :

1. Medallion windows.
2. Figure windows.
3. Rose windows.
4. Jesse windows.
5. Simple white pattern windows.

1. *Medallion Windows.*—These were usually but not invariably placed in the aisles of a church (as at Canterbury), so that their subjects could be easily deciphered. The windows themselves were of the usual Norman type, wide single openings with semicircular heads.[2]

---

[1] [See paper by F. Sydney Eden in *The Journal of the British Society of Master Glass-Painters*, No. 3 (October 1925), p. 20.]

[2] For architectural details readers may consult *Parish Church Architecture*, by E. Tyrrell-Green in this series.

As noted above, their subjects consisted for the most part of Old and New Testament incidents, but scenes from the lives of the saints occurred as well; for instance, at Dorchester Abbey, where are four small medallions depicting incidents in the life of St. Birinus.

The windows contained a varying number of pictures, each set within a framework of massive iron bent to the required shape; circles, semicircles, squares, or other such designs, the glass being held in position by means of strong wedges. The panels themselves were entirely mosaic in principle, being made up of a large number of small pieces, over fifty perhaps to the square foot, each laboriously chipped into shape by means of the grozing iron, and all leaded together to make a complete picture. The design was entirely determined by the leadlines, the painting being secondary, consisting indeed of little more than strong outlines shaded off by a semi-transparent half-tone wash.

The figures in these panels were tall, slim, and badly proportioned, their faces and, in fact, all flesh parts being painted on brown pot-metals. These heads, though certainly the reverse of beautiful, judged by our modern standards, were strongly drawn, the face oval, the eyes large and staring, the mouth small, and the line of the nose continued upwards to form the eyebrows. The hair, which was short and curly, was drawn upon the same piece of glass as the head, not on a separate portion, as was often the case with fourteenth-century glass. Haloes were always on separate pieces of glass, and usually coloured. Hands and feet were badly drawn, the former resembling rakes or combs. The draperies of secular figures consisted of a close-fitting garment reaching to the knees, the sleeves sometimes reaching to the wrists, sometimes to the elbows, with under-sleeves of another colour. Over this long robe was a loose-fitting mantle fastened on the left shoulder by a clasp or brooch, the various folds being delineated by lines and curves. The legs were covered by boots and long coloured stockings.

Ecclesiastical figures wore the chasuble over dalmatic and alb, episcopal persons wearing low-pointed mitres. Military figures wore chain mail with steel caps on their heads, being armed with sword, spear, or axe, and carrying kite-shaped shields. Regal figures wore a long tunic reaching to the ankles, and over it a mantle of another colour. Their crowns were of yellow pot-metal and very low. There was very little attempt at scenery. Indoor scenes were indicated by a line of arches; an exterior by a building or a tree or two. The colours employed for both draperies and architectural details were chiefly ruby, green, white, maroon, and yellow pot-metals. The backgrounds of these medallions were usually deep blue, often showing a marked purple tone, although at Dorchester Abbey both green and red were used for backgrounds. All backgrounds in this first period were perfectly plain, devoid of any diaper patterns.

All colours employed were very deep and intensely rich in tone, their shades varying very greatly, owing to the inexperience of the makers in mixing the ingredients. The ruby, for instance, was often very streaky in quality and extraordinarily luminous, the blues being frequently of a strongly purple tone, while the white ranged in colour from green to yellowish, often having a horny appearance. All glass of this period was very thick and uneven in quality, which added to its sparkle.

Some idea of the varied colour scheme in these twelfth-century medallions may be gathered from the description given of one of those at Canterbury Cathedral in a recently published book.[1] The panel in question represents the Conversion of the Heathen (Fig. 13). " The heathen (in white, green, red, and yellow), in spite of the efforts of a devil (dull red with green wings) in the air, desert a temple containing an idol (pale blue against red background) behind an altar (gold, blue top), and follow Christ (red cross nimbus, pink

[1] *Mediæval England* (Oxford, 1924), p. 494.

mantle) mounting the steps (green) of a church (red roof) with its altar (gold, white top) and font (purple). The background is blue."

The subjects in these medallion windows were explained to the educated beholder by means of Latin inscriptions in the type of lettering known as " Lombardic " (see p. 88), which was very much easier to decipher than the contracted " black-letter " which superseded it about 1375. Such inscriptions were obtained by covering a strip of glass with tracing pigment, and then picking out the letters with a pointed stick. They were usually set at top and at bottom if square ; if circular or semicircular, then round the edges or in a line near the base.

There was generally an outer border of thin strips of coloured glass, sometimes painted to imitate beading or other forms of ornament, and often arranged in several layers, each of a different colour. These pictorial medallions were set upon a background of stiff conventional foliate patterns, also purely mosaic in principle, and executed in various colours, their backgrounds being arranged so as to counterchange with those of the medallions. The whole window was surrounded by very wide borders of elaborately designed repeats of foliate character, executed in white and coloured glass, and set upon blue or ruby within thin strips of colours.

2. *Figure Windows.*—The figure windows of this period, which were usually set in the clerestories, contained tall, badly proportioned, ungainly figures with long arms, usually arranged two in an opening, one above the other. At Canterbury the clerestories were filled with the Ancestry of Christ ; whilst those of the twelfth-century choir in York Minster apparently contained ecclesiastics, of whom one only, an archbishop, has been preserved. These figures were clad in tight-fitting coloured robes of the same type as those in the small medallion pictures, and were usually seated upon variously coloured stools or benches intended

by their designers to represent thrones. Their names
were painted on large bands of glass, being sometimes
set beneath their feet, in other cases crossing the
background near their heads. The backgrounds were
generally of plain blue (Fig. 14). Sometimes these
figures were surmounted by simple arches, or even by
canopies of a very primitive type, consisting of little
more than a small turret, rising from a flat tiled roof,
as in the York figure panel; or they might be set within
ovals or quatrefoils, bordered with strips of coloured
glass arranged in several rows, the whole placed, like
the medallions, upon coloured foliate fields within
wide borders.

3. *Rose Windows.*—These were of rare occurrence
in England, and the only example of twelfth-century
date to retain its original glazing was that in the north
choir transept of Canterbury Cathedral, a quatrefoil-
shaped opening within a circle, the centre being made
up of a framework of massive iron. The subject, now
imperfect, was that of the Old Law, Moses in the centre
holding the Tables of the Law, accompanied by a
figure representing the Synagogue holding the Levitical
books. These two figures were placed beneath simple
arches within a square. Around them were four of
the Cardinal Virtues: (top) Justice, stooping and holding
in her right hand a pair of scales over a golden bag;
(left) Prudence (?), holding a winged serpent in one
hand and a dove in the other (Matt. x. 16); (right)
Temperance, holding a lighted torch and a cup;
(bottom) Fortitude, holding a sword, about to slay
a green dragon. "These pictures form two squares,
the one inscribed in the other. The outer square
is inscribed in a circle, the external segments of which
contain, with beautiful arabesques of blue and green
and white, pictures of the four Great Prophets, Isaiah
and Jeremiah leaning forward on their thrones, and
Ezekiel and Daniel reclining." Probably the Minor
Prophets, now lost, were in the outer circle.

4. *Tree of Jesse Windows.*—These were very simple

in plan at this early date, containing some half-dozen figures at most, very different from the elaborate schemes of the fourteenth century, when this particular design may be said to have reached its zenith. No perfect *English* example remains to-day, although a panel taken from one is still preserved in a window of York Minster. It is necessary, therefore, to take a description from that of a window also painted by Frenchmen, but for a French cathedral, that of Chartres.

" At the base is the recumbent figure of Jesse ; the straight stem of the tree proceeding from him is almost entirely hidden by a string of figures, one above the other, occupying the central part of the window and represented as kings ; above them sits the Virgin, also crowned ; and on the arch of the window sits Our Lord in Majesty, surrounded by seven doves to signify the Gifts of the Spirit. It is not perhaps quite clear upon what these figures sit. They hold on with both hands to branches of highly conventional Roman-esque foliage, springing from the main stem, and occupy-ing the space about the figures in very ornamental fashion. A series of half-medallions on either side of this central design contains little figures of attendant prophets, in a sense the spiritual ancestors of the Saviour. All this is in the deepest and richest mosaic colour in the beautiful bluish Jesse window at the west end of the cathedral of Chartres, which belongs to the middle of the twelfth century." [1]

The panel remaining at York Minster agrees exactly with the above description. " It was," says Professor Lethaby, " about 2 feet 4 inches square ; the colour was deep and splendid ; the ground blue, the foliage red, yellow, and green, and the strong scrolling stalks of the ' tree ' white. The King who occupied this section was largely vested in green and brown-purple, and his shoes were red. Mr. Westlake (an eminent authority upon mediæval painted glass) thought that

---

[1] Lewis Day, *Windows : a Book about Stained and Painted Glass,* 3rd ed. (London, 1909), p. 350.

it was either copied from or designed by an artist educated in the same school which produced the Jesse tree at Chartres."[1]

This panel was bordered with a repeat of hexagonal frames each filled with stiff conventional foliage, the interstices being filled in the same manner and the whole set upon a coloured field.

5. *Pattern Windows.*—The fifth type of twelfth-century glass painting, though very simple in design, was in some respects by far the most interesting, as it foreshadowed the "*grisaille*" or grey-pattern windows of the next century. Moreover, it is exceedingly valuable as showing the type of design used in glazing a small country parish church in that early period. The only example of this type remaining in England is that in Brabourne Church, Kent. It consists merely of "simple pattern work carried out in clear glass, relieved with colour in the backgrounds and in the central ornaments, and represents a floral design placed within half-circles, all which is devoid of pigment except for a centre of quatrefoil situated between outer margins of lateral semicircles."[2]

It should be added that in this first period of glass painting no attempt was made to introduce conventional portrait figures, kneeling or otherwise, of the donors of glass; neither had heraldry come into use as a window subject.

[1] *Archæological Journal*, lxxii (1915), p. 40.
[2] Nelson, pp. 102–3.

CHAPTER VII

EARLY ENGLISH GLASS (1200–1280)

TOWARDS the end of the twelfth century the massive Norman architecture began to change by slow degrees into what is popularly termed "Early English," or more correctly, Early Gothic, the round-headed windows of the former period gradually giving place to graceful pointed lancets, at first single, but later, in the thirteenth century, arranged in pairs, triplets, or even larger groups.

This change of architectural style was a very gradual one, some architects being more conservative than others, or perhaps finding themselves unable to assimilate new ideas. The result was that in some cases, as in the Trinity Chapel of Canterbury Cathedral, some windows remained round-headed, even though the arcades supporting the clerestories above had changed to pointed.

At first this change of architecture made but little difference to the glass painters. Indeed, it is often difficult to give a precise date to glass painted about the end of the twelfth century, some designers, like the architects with whom they collaborated, being more advanced in style than others.

All glass of this period may for convenience be divided into six classes :

1. Medallion windows.
2. Figure windows.
3. Rose windows.
4. Jesse windows.
5. Grisaille windows.
6. Combination of medallions with grisaille.

1. *Medallion Windows.*—In principle of design the medallion windows of the early thirteenth century differed but little from those already described, and, like them, were usually placed in the aisles of a church as near to the eye as possible. Their subjects, however, differed considerably from those of the twelfth century, for in addition to Old and New Testament scenes they depicted incidents from the lives of well-known saints. At Canterbury Cathedral, for example, the twelve windows of the retro-choir, glazed early in the thirteenth century, were all once filled with an elaborate series of medallions depicting miracles worked by the intercession of St. Thomas of Canterbury, the martyred archbishop whose magnificent shrine stood in the centre of this part of the church. Six of these windows still remain in a somewhat restored condition, other windows of this date in the same cathedral retaining fragments of a series depicting the life and martyrdom of St. Alphege. All this glass dates from about 1230.

Again, at Lincoln Minster, where was once much early thirteenth-century medallion glass, the subjects still remaining include Miracles of the Virgin Mary, St. Nicholas, and St. John the Evangelist, as well as of New and Old Testament series, while lesser portions of other series remain in Salisbury Cathedral and Westminster Abbey.

As noted above, these medallions differed very little in principle of design from those of the twelfth century, being still purely mosaic in treatment. Their colours were perhaps a little less intense, the drawing of the figures and other details a little better in quality, folds of draperies, for instance, being more flowing and less angular. The backgrounds, which were still nearly always blue, were occasionally diapered with a scroll pattern produced by laying on a wash of pigment and picking out the required design with a stick or brush, as in a window of the Trinity Chapel of Canterbury Cathedral. Attempts were occasionally made at realistic treatment, heads of martyrs, for instance,

being painted upon pieces of streaky ruby in order to
show the effects of wounds, as in a fine panel depicting
the Stoning of St. Stephen, now in Grateley Church,
Hampshire, but originally forming part of the glazing
of Salisbury Cathedral.

This Grateley panel is interesting as showing the
arrangement and treatment of a mid-thirteenth-century
picture medallion. The subject, as noted above, is
the Martyrdom of St. Stephen, the picture being set
within a circle surrounded by a lozenge. On the right,
the saint, vested in deep purple-blue dalmatic with
dull yellow fringes, green maniple, and white alb, is
collapsing sideways to the ground. His face is painted
on a piece of streaky ruby, intended to represent the
effect of wounds received; he is tonsured, and has a
green halo. In the centre is a man clad in short green
tunic, who points at the saint whilst turning to address
a second man, who, clad in brown mantle over green
tunic, with red hose, seems to express his disappoint-
ment at having arrived too late. The features of both
these miscreants are markedly Jewish in type. On
the right of the group is a small light green tree; the
background is blue. Beneath is the inscription in
white Lombardic characters picked out of a "matt"
field: "Step(hanu)s orans expirat" ("Stephen praying
dies"). The border is ruby with a thin outer ring of
greenish-white beading. The spandrels formed by the
intersection of circle with lozenge are filled in with
coloured foliage on a ruby field. These medallions
differed considerably in shape from those of the previous
century, the iron frames supporting them being bent
into various elaborate designs, such as quatrefoils,
intersected by saltires, lozenges interspaced by pairs
of circles, and so forth.

The backgrounds on which these pictures were placed
varied in design, sometimes consisting of coloured
foliage on ruby, sometimes of a mosaic diaper, blue
squares each painted with a simple pattern outlined
in leadwork with a small red circle at each corner.

Examples of both types occur at Canterbury and
Lincoln. The borders, too, were not so wide as those
of the previous century; moreover, the foliage showed
a slight tendency towards naturalistic treatment.

A singular and unusual treatment of a window was
that formerly existing at Lanchester Church (Durham),
where are three late twelfth- or early thirteenth-century
square panels depicting respectively the Angel's Annunciation to the Shepherds, the Adoration of the
Magi, and the Flight into Egypt, the drawing and
general technique differing very markedly from anything
at Canterbury. These panels, with others now lost,
seem originally to have filled the central lancet of the
triplet east window. Each panel was separated from
the next by two thick fleshy white stems, each divided
into three branches, making six in all. Four of these
branches rose into the picture, terminating in flowers;
the remaining two turned downwards so as to occupy
the lower courses of each panel. The background of
this scroll work was ruby, thus counter-changing with
the blue fields of the panels themselves. No traces
remain of the glass once in the side lancets; neither
are these three panels now in their original place.[1]

2. *Figure Windows.*—Although no perfect example
remains of a figure window of this period, sundry odd
panels from a series are collected in the east windows
of the choir aisles at Lincoln Minster. These panels,
which contain figures of kings and apostles placed
within elongated quatrefoils, are enough to show that
the early figure windows of the thirteenth century did
not differ materially in design and treatment from those
of the previous century, while, like them, they were
placed in the clerestories of a great church.

3. *Rose Windows.*—The only example of a thirteenth-
century rose window retaining its original glazing, or
at least the greater part of it, is that in the north transept
of Lincoln Minster, the famous " Dean's Eye," measuring

24 feet in diameter. It differed considerably in plan from the earlier window at Canterbury, in that the various panels were set each within a framework of stone instead of iron bars, thus giving the whole the appearance of a glorified medallion window. The subject originally depicted was the Last Judgment, but there are now several alien insertions, although mostly of contemporary date.

4. *Jesse Windows.*—Here, again, no perfect example remains of this subject, but existing fragments in Salisbury Cathedral,[1] Lincoln Minster, and Westwell Church, Kent, show that although still comparatively simple in design, they were much more advanced in style of drawing and general technique than the stiff archaic earlier types. The Jesse trees of the thirteenth century still seem for the most part to have been confined to a single lancet; although it is possible that the Salisbury Tree of Jesse was placed in a pair of lancets set side by side. The figures were usually seated, being placed within ovals of plain blue or ruby, outlined in foliage, which, though still of a conventional type and bearing little resemblance to a vine, was more graceful and flowing in style. The leaves were trefoil or cinque-foil, small bunches of fruit appearing here and there, while the backgrounds of the lights usually counter-changed in colour with those of the ovals.

But all these coloured windows had two serious drawbacks. They made the churches very dark, and, by reason of the labour expended in making up their elaborate mosaics, they were so costly that only the richest ecclesiastics or noblemen could afford to pay for them. And so about the year 1250 these elaborate mosaic windows were gradually abandoned in favour of the pattern type known as—

5. *Grisaille* (from the French *gris*, grey).—At first the designs in these grisaille windows were very simple,

---

[1] The Salisbury fragments have been recently removed from the west window of the nave and placed in a nave aisle window, where they are nearer to the eye.

as witness an early example at Stockbury Church, Kent, of about 1250.[1] It originally filled a single lancet and consisted of quatrefoils filled out with conventional foliage on cross-hatched fields, set on lozenges of blue glass, and bordered alternately with red and yellow. Between each pair of coloured lozenges was a leaded one partly overlapped by them and filled in with foliage of the same type as that in the quatrefoils.

From such simple designs, which were but a slight improvement upon the twelfth-century example at Brabourne, Kent (see page 67), more and more elaborate patterns were evolved until windows were filled with schemes comprising six or seven layers of circles and lozenges all arranged so as to overlap or intersect one another, some of these shapes being bordered by thin strips of coloured glass, others merely outlined in leadwork, but one and all filled in with graceful and ornate foliate patterns, which, as the century advanced, showed an ever-increasing tendency on the part of their designers to turn from conventional to naturalistic treatment. Sometimes these patterns were set upon cross-hatched backgrounds, sometimes merely painted in outline, but in every case they were drawn in strong sweeping curves with black oxidised pigment, no attempt being made to soften the edges or otherwise introduce shading.

A feature of these grisaille windows was that in practically every case the foliage was confined within the limits of the shapes wherein it was painted, and not, as in the next period, allowed to sweep unchecked over half the light. An exception to this practice did, however, occur at York Minster, where five huge lancets, each 53 feet high by 5 feet wide, the famous " Five Sisters," were all filled with thirteenth-century grisaille (Fig. 15). In these " the leaf-work is remarkable, since it tends to stray outside the limits of the containing panels."[2]

[1] Illustrated in Winston, *Hints*, etc., vol. ii, plate 4.
[2] Nelson, p. 250.

It should be noted that though all or practically all these foliate designs were confined within a given space, they no longer strictly followed the leadlines and so form the germ of that which ultimately (in the seventeenth century) brought about the downfall of good glass painting, namely, the elimination of leadlines from the design.   The best examples of this first type of grisaille remaining in England are in Salisbury Cathedral,[1] York Minster, and Lincoln Minster.   Smaller portions also remain in a north transept window of Westminster Abbey.

Another type of grisaille, an example of which formerly existed at Westwell in Kent, consisted of quarries, each bearing a leaf-shaped pattern set on cross-hatched fields within a white outlined border, the lower third of certain quarries being cut away to admit of a fan-shaped piece of coloured glass being inserted.   The whole light was bordered with foliage painted upon white, set upon coloured fields.[2]

A simpler type of grisaille consisted of slips of plain unpainted glass relieved by small pieces of colour set at intervals, the whole leaded into interlacing patterns of an elaborate nature.   Examples of this type occur at Salisbury Cathedral and at Westminster Abbey.

The borders of these grisaille windows, though still composed entirely of pot-metal glass, were much thinner and simpler in principle of design, usually consisting of repeats of foliage, some in white *on* colour, others in white and colour alternately, set on ruby or blue fields, and like the foliage in the body of the lights showing more and more tendency to naturalistic treatment as the century advanced.   Usually these coloured borders were separated from the stonework by a narrow strip of greenish white.

All these grisaille windows varied very greatly in hue, sea-green, olive, grey-green, and light (almost yellow) green being among the shades found, while the

[1] See Nelson, plates 14 and 15.
[2] Winston, *Hints*, vol. ii, plate 1.   See also Nelson, p. 15.

oxidised pigment often imparted a brownish tone to the whole window, especially if cross-hatching had been employed as a groundwork.

But such designs, though beautiful from the designer's point of view, were uninteresting to the general public. And so about 1270 we find glass painters beginning to adorn their grisaille windows with picture subjects, placing them at intervals down the centre of a light, or in the case of a small window about half-way down. The shapes of these panels varied according to taste or requirements. Sometimes they consisted of circles, pointed ovals, or quatrefoils, as at Chetwode in Buckinghamshire, Stanton St. John in Oxfordshire, and Salisbury Cathedral; sometimes of oblongs with trefoil-heads, as at Stanton Harcourt (Oxon).[1] The subjects represented were either single figures of apostles, saints, or ecclesiastics, or Scriptural scenes, the latter as a rule being singularly lifeless, and often quite lacking the spirited animation of the earlier medallions.

These medallions and figure panels differed somewhat from those painted earlier in the period, being simpler in construction, and made up of fewer and therefore much larger pieces of glass. For this reason two or three heads were sometimes painted on a single piece of glass, as in a panel depicting the Massacre of the Innocents now in the Jerusalem Chamber of Westminster Abbey. The figures themselves were tall and more graceful, their robes being now made to hang more loosely about their bodies, thus containing fewer folds. These draperies were much simpler, usually consisting of a loose mantle of one colour worn over one shoulder, beneath it a gown or tunic of a second colour, legs and feet being bare. Ecclesiastics such as bishops wore a pointed chasuble over a dalmatic and alb, the pallium worn by an archbishop being painted on the chasuble, as in the case of a figure at East Tytherley, Hants. The mitres are very low (see Fig. 21).

[1] Winston, *Hints*, vol. ii, plate 5.

Military figures were clad in chain-mail, as in the earlier medallions. The attitudes of these figures began to display a slight S-like curve, which has been compared to that of a person standing on one leg and leaning backwards. It became much more marked in the next period (see Chapter VIII).

The brownish pink still used for all flesh tones was of a much lighter hue. Features showed a marked improvement in delineation, shading being occasionally introduced, but hair was still drawn on the same piece of glass. Haloes when represented were leaded on separately. Architectural details such as arches were occasionally introduced into medallions, as in a circle at Salisbury Cathedral, where a king and a bishop stand side by side, each under a simple arch. Backgrounds were still plain blue or ruby, but small conventional ornaments were sometimes leaded in at intervals. The borders of these pictures were much thinner, usually consisting of one or two layers of glass, either white or coloured, the outer one being sometimes enriched with an elaborate diaper pattern, as at Chetwode, Bucks.

The grisaille fields on which these panels were set differed little in principle of construction from earlier examples, except that the " leadwork pattern " type fell into disuse. Their foliage designs showed, however, an increasing tendency to turn from conventional to naturalistic treatment, as did their borders, which were now much thinner. In short, the style was making rapid progress towards the next change, that of the " Decorated " period, 1280–1350.

About 1270 heraldry had begun to make its appearance as a form of window decoration, its gay tones adding appreciably in colour to the still somewhat monotonous pattern windows, while often affording in itself most valuable information as to the approximate date of the glass itself. At first the shields, which were of the earlier " heater " shape, that is, with sides curving inwards continuously from their tops, bore very simple charges, one coat-of-arms only in each. The Royal Arms of England at this time consisted of three golden lions or " leopards " on a ruby field only, those of France, azure semé of fleur-de-lys or (that is, a blue field powdered with golden fleur-de-lys) being shown always on a separate shield. Such shields, whatever their device, were usually placed near the bottom of a light, and embedded in the grisaille without any intervening border. Portrait figures of donors had not yet made their appearance in English windows, while all inscriptions were still in Lombardic characters and produced as before.

CHAPTER VIII

THE DECORATED PERIOD (1280–1350)

DURING the changes described in the latter part of the last chapter, architecture was undergoing a gradual evolution from the Early English into the Decorated style, with the result that windows began to be made up of two or more lights within one arch, the main lights terminating in acutely pointed trefoil or cinque-foil heads, and the upper part being subdivided so as to form tracery openings. At first these smaller openings were of the type known as *geometrical*, con-sisting entirely of various combinations of the circle, such as the trefoil, quatrefoil, cinquefoil, etc. Later, this simple type developed into that known as *cur-vilinear*, where the traceries were formed by ogees or flowing lines, so becoming much more ornate and complicated in design.

All glass paintings of the Decorated period may for convenience be divided into five distinct types, each of which had its own peculiar characteristics, though conforming in general detail one with another. Types 3, 4, and 5 continued in general use right through the fourteenth century, greatly improving in style as the century advanced.

The five types were :
1. Ornamental grisaille.
2. Small panels on grisaille.
3. Figure or subject and canopy windows.
4. Single figures upon quarries.
5. Jesse windows.

1. *Ornamental Grisaille.*—At first the grisaille window of the Decorated period differed very little if at all

in principle of construction from that of late Early English, the elaborate repeat of interlaced leaded and coloured strapwork being retained. There were, however, two differences in the design : (1) the earlier cross-hatched backgrounds were dispensed with ; (2) naturalistic treatment of foliage definitely replaced conventional. The latter took time to disappear, some designers evidently being more conservative than others, for the foliage in some grisaille at Exeter Cathedral painted (to judge by the evidence of the Cathedral Fabric Rolls) as late as 1300–10 was still very largely conventional in treatment. But, generally speaking, by 1290 elaborate schemes were being produced based upon oak, vine, ivy, maple, hawthorn, and other forms of plant life. These designs were no longer rigidly contained within the ovals, circles, or other shapes, but were intertwined with and around them, as at Norbury Church, Derbyshire, and at Chartham Church, Kent. At first the subjects set in these *grisaille* windows were of a very simple nature, consisting of little more than shields or roundels containing grotesque or coloured geometrical patterns set at intervals down the lights. At Norbury a large shield was placed near the top of each main light in the eight side windows (each of three lights) of the chancel, while in some early glass of this type in the Chapel of St. Gabriel and St. Mary Magdalene in Exeter Cathedral a shield was placed in the centre of every middle panel of a light, while every bottom panel had in its centre a pair of keys, the emblem of St. Peter, the patron saint of that cathedral.[1] The shields agreed very closely in type with those mentioned at the end of the last chapter, and like them bore single coats only.

But the designers soon wearied of these grisaille windows and cast about for new ideas. The elaborate interlaced patterns of coloured strapwork were therefore abandoned, and the windows made up into " quarries " (from the French *carré*, a diamond), on which foliate

[1] Bishop and Prideaux, *The Building of Exeter Cathedral*, p. 148.

designs could be painted in graceful curves and scrolls sweeping over the entire surface of each light, as in Merton College Chapel, the Chapter House of York Minster, and formerly in the choir aisles of Exeter Cathedral. In each of these three cases the foliage springs from a central tree trunk, which at York issued from the head of a monster, half animal and half fish, placed at the foot of each light.

The glass itself was sometimes divided into a large number of small pieces of different sizes and shapes, but so arranged that when leaded together they formed an elaborate interlacing pattern. In other cases it was made up of the lozenge-shaped pieces termed " quarries," as at White Notley in Essex and at Stanton Harcourt. But in either case the foliate patterns were allowed to trail over the leaded fields, being so arranged that every individual portion of glass bore its own distinct section of stem or spray of foliage, so that the existence of even two or three such fragments in a Decorated window to-day may still tell, to the expert eye, their tale of what has been.

It was often the practice to draw an outlined border (technically termed " strapwork ") around the whole or even a part of each piece of glass ; if of quarry shape, usually on its two upper edges only, so that the whole when leaded up presented the appearance of trellis work with climbing plants growing over it. A variation upon these trailing foliate fields is found at Stapleford Abbots (Essex), and Mottisfont (Hants), where each quarry bore its own separate leaf drawn in outline and placed within a half-border.

In every case, be the type of foliage what it might, the designs were drawn in strong, firm outline, some of the veins of the leaves being indicated, but no attempt was made to round off edges by shading, while, as already noted, the cross-hatched backgrounds were discontinued.

It should also be noted that these windows were often glazed in pairs opposite one another in the aisles

Photo F. H. Crossley

FIG. 1.   BRISTOL CATHEDRAL.   FIFTEENTH CENTURY HEAD.

SHOWING USE OF YELLOW STAIN FOR HAIR, CROWN AND HALO.

FIG. 3. MEDIÆVAL GLASS-MAKING.

MINIATURE FROM A 15TH CENT. MS. IN THE BRITISH MUSEUM. (ADD. MS. 24189).

From Salzmann's *Mediæval English Industries*, by permission of the Clarendon Press.

FIG. 4.   MODEL OF A WHITEWASHED TABLF.

BY MR. J. A. KNOWLES.

The medallion of the Scourging, which is being set out, is from a modern
drawing in 12th cent. style in O. Merson's *Les Vitraux* (fig. 113).

FIG. 7. YORK MINSTER. ST. WILLIAM WINDOW.
A BOY HEALED AT THE SHRINE OF ST. WILLIAM.

FIG. 8. YORK MINSTER. ST. WILLIAM WINDOW.
A LEPER WOMAN HEALED AT THE SHRINE OF ST. WILLIAM.

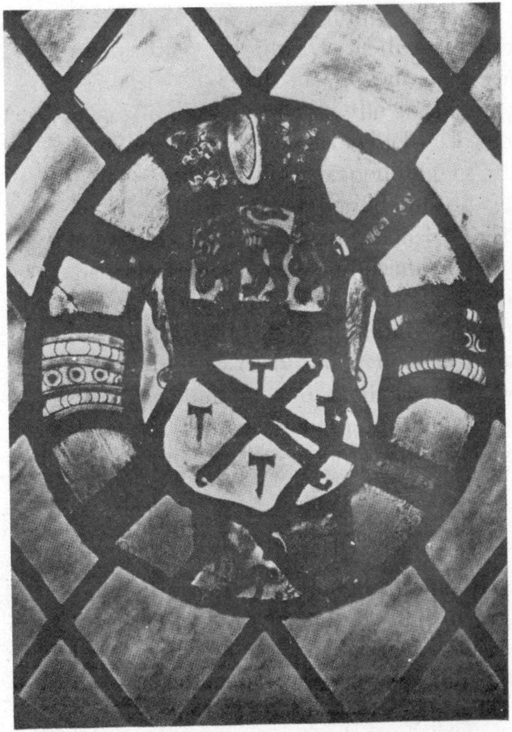

Photo J. A. Knowles

FIG. 9. ARMS OF THE YORK GLASS-PAINTERS' GILD IN ST. HELEN'S CHURCH, YORK.

SHOWING GROZING IRONS AND CLOSING OR GLAZING NAILS.

Photo S. A. Pitcher

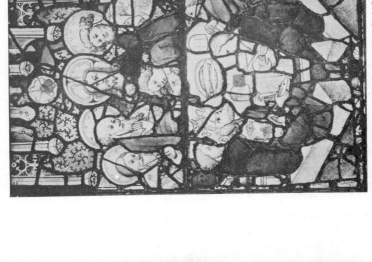

FIG. 10. GREAT MALVERN, EAST WINDOW.

THE LAST SUPPER.

FIG. 12. GRESFORD, EAST WINDOW.

THE PRESENTATION OF MARY IN THE TEMPLE.

FIG. 11. ST. PETER MANCROFT, NORWICH, EAST WINDOW.

ADORATION OF THE SHEPHERDS.

3. 14. CANTERBURY CATHEDRAL.

METHUSELAH.

FIG. 13. CANTERBURY CATHEDRAL.

THE CONVERSION OF THE HEATHEN.

From a 12th cent. window in the north aisle of the choir.

Photo J. A. Knowles

FIG. 15. YORK MINSTER.

ONE COMPARTMENT OF THE "FIVE SISTERS" WINDOW.

From J. Browne's *York Minster*.

FIG. 16. DEERHURST.

ST. CATHERINE.

FIG. 17. TEWKESBURY.

CANOPY FROM ONE OF THE CHOIR
WINDOWS.

Photo W. M. Dodson

FIG. 19. EAST WINDOW, SELLING CHURCH.

Photo W. M. Dodson

FIG. 20. MORPETH, EAST WINDOW OF SOUTH AISLE.

CHRIST IN MAJESTY, ST. BLAISE, ST. DENIS.

FIG. 21. CREDENHILL. FIGURES ON QUARRY-BACKGROUNDS.

ST. THOMAS OF CANTERBURY AND ST. THOMAS CANTILUPE.

Photo S. A. Pitcher

FIG. 22. GLOUCESTER CATHEDRAL, EAST WINDOW.

SHIELD OF RICHARD LORD TALBOT (GULES A LION RAMPANT WITHIN A BORDURE ENGRAILED OR).

Photo F. H. Crossley

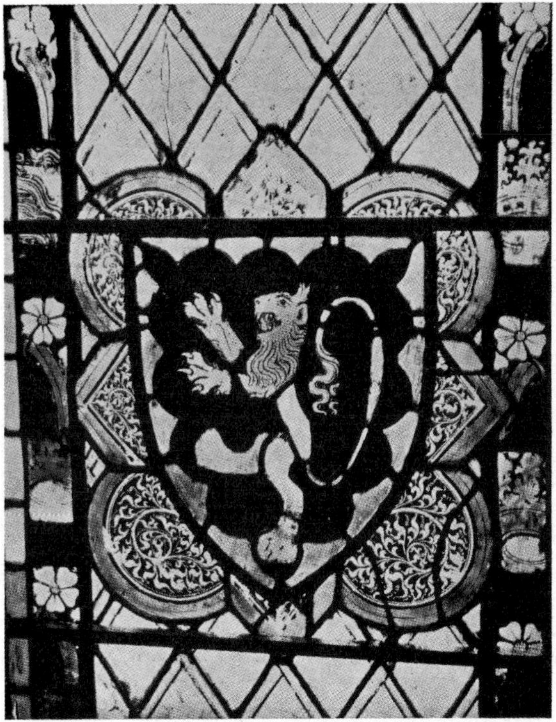

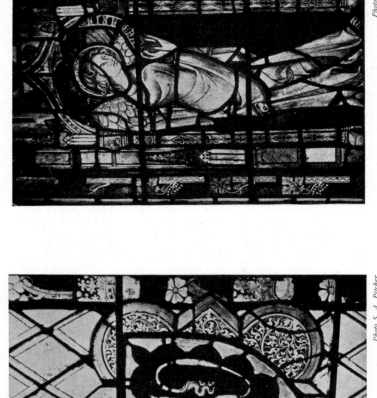

FIG. 23. OXFORD CATHEDRAL.

GABRIEL, FROM AN ANNUNCIATION IN THE LATIN CHAPEL.

Photo Victoria and Albert Museum

FIG. 24. THREE LIGHTS FROM WINCHESTER COLLEGE CHAPEL, NOW IN THE VICTORIA AND ALBERT MUSEUM.

ST. JOHN THE EVANGELIST, SOPHONIAS (ZEPHANIAH), ST. JAMES THE GREAT.

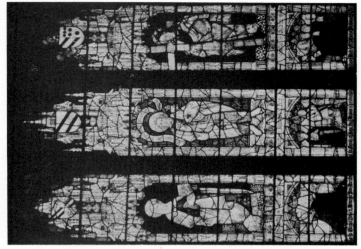

Photo F. H. Crossley

FIG. 27. ALMONDBURY. EAST WINDOW OF NORTH CHAPEL.

ST. ELIZABETH, ST. JOHN THE BAPTIST, ST. HELEN. DONORS BELOW. SHIELDS OF ARMS IN THE CANOPIES.

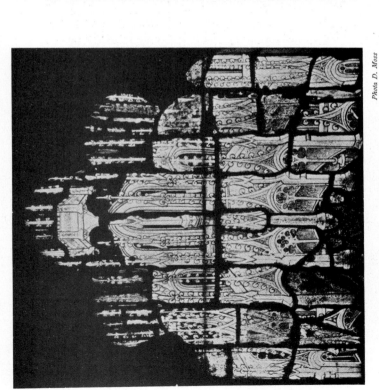

Photo D. Moss

FIG. 26. CIRENCESTER CHURCH. A 15TH CENTURY CANOPY.

FIG. 20. ST. THOMAS RECOGNIZING THE RISEN CHRIST.

FROM A WINDOW IN THE NORTH AISLE OF ALL SAINTS, NORTH STREET, YORK.

FIG. 28. WELLS CATHEDRAL.

HEAD OF ST. ERKENWALD IN THE TRACERY OF A WINDOW IN THE RETRO-QUIRE.

Photo W. M. Dodson

FIG. 30. LUDLOW CHURCH, ST. JOHN'S CHAPEL. THE PALMERS' WINDOW.

Photo W. M. Dodson

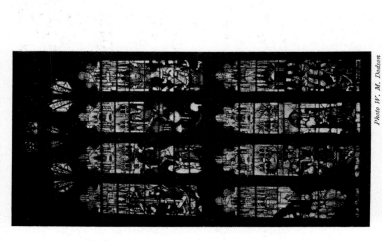

FIG. 31. GRESFORD CHURCH, EAST WINDOW.

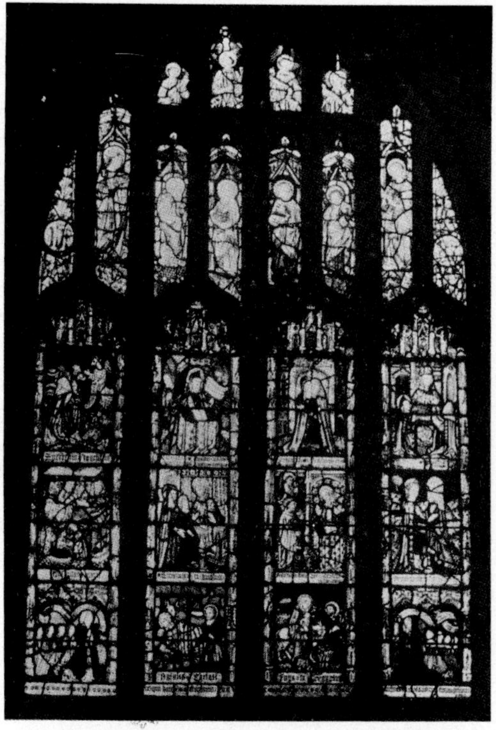

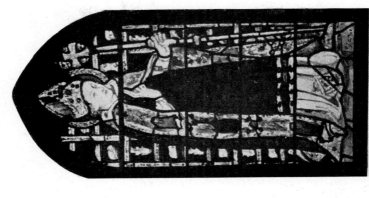

FIG. 33. ST. THOMAS OF CANTERBURY. EAST WINDOW OF THE BEAUCHAMP CHAPEL, WARWICK.

Photo W. M. Dodson

FIG. 32. CLAVERING.

ST. CATHERINE DISPUTING WITH THE PHILOSOPHERS.

Photo F. H. Crossley

FIG. 35.   WINSCOMBE. EAST WINDOW OF NORTH AISLE.

THE CRUCIFIXION, ST. ANTONY, AND DONORS.

Photo W. M. Dodson

FIG. 34.   ST. CATHERINE, ST. JOHN THE BAPTIST, AND ST. CHRISTOPHER.

FROM A WINDOW IN ST. JOHN'S CHAPEL, LUDLOW CHURCH.

Photo W. M. Dodson

FIG. 36. MARGARETTING, EAST WINDOW. JESSE TREE.

Photo F. H. Crossley

FIG. 38. ALMONDBURY CHURCH, EAST WINDOW OF NORTH
CHAPEL (*see* FIG. 27).

A DONOR OF THE KAYE FAMILY WITH HIS WIFE.

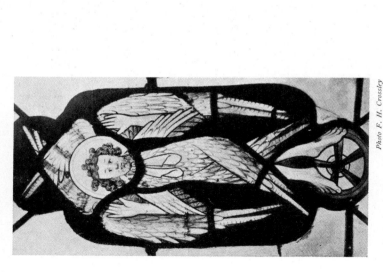

Photo F. H. Crossley

FIG. 37. VARNTON. FEATHERED
ANGEL STANDING ON A WHEEL.

FIG. 39.   CIRENCESTER, WEST WINDOW.
WHITE-ROBED ANGELS PLAYING BAGPIPES AND PORTABLE ORGAN.

FIG. 40.   WINSCOMBE.   KNEELING DONORS IN EAST WINDOW OF
NORTH AISLE.

Photo J. P. Clarke

FIG. 41.   KING'S COLLEGE CHAPEL, CAMBRIDGE.   LOWER HALF OF
A WINDOW ON THE SOUTH SIDE.

THE UNBELIEF OF THOMAS, AND CHRIST APPEARING TO THE APOSTLES.   IN THE MIDDLE
A PROPHET AND AN ANGEL HOLDING TEXTS.

Photo H.M. Stationery Office

FIG. 43. HENRY VII'S CHAPEL, WESTMINSTER.

ANGELS HOLDING SHIELDS WITH INITIALS OF HENRY VII AND ELIZABETH.

Photo S. A. Pitcher

FIG. 44. LYDIARD TREGOZE. 17TH CENTURY GLASS.

ST. JOHN THE BAPTIST AND ST. JOHN THE EVANGELIST.

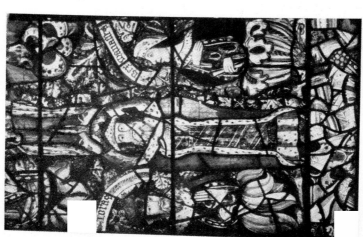

Photo F. H. Crossley

FIG. 42. DYSERTH. PART OF THE JESSE WINDOW.

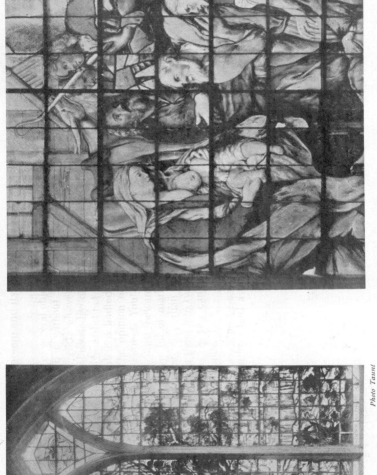

FIG. 46. CHAPEL OF THE VYNE, HAMPSHIRE.

ADORATION OF THE SHEPHERDS, BY JOHN ROWELL (1770), FROM A WINDOW IN THE TOMB CHAMBER.

See C. W. Chute, *A History of the Vyne*, p. 150.

FIG. 45. OXFORD CATHEDRAL.
JONAH WINDOW.

Photo S. A. Pitcher

FIG. 48. WINCHESTER COLLEGE CHAPEL, EAST WINDOW.

KING ABIJAH.

Copy of original glass by Betton & Evans.

Photo W. M. Dodson

FIG. 47. VICTORIA AND ALBERT MUSEUM.

KING JOASH, ONE OF THE ORIGINAL FIGURES FROM THE EAST WINDOW OF WINCHESTER COLLEGE CHAPEL.

Photo S. A. Pitcher

FIG. 50. THE MAYOR'S PARLOUR IN THE OLD
TOWN HALL, LEICESTER.

ROUNDEL OF SEPTEMBER: THRESHING WHEAT.

Photo W. M. Dodson

FIG. 49. ROUNDEL OF THE RESUR-
RECTION FROM AN OLD HOUSE IN
LEICESTER.

Now in the Leicester Museum.

FIG. 51. QUARRIES IN YARNTON CHURCH.

LEFT, A HEN WITH "GREETE, RICHLYNG, GREETE." RIGHT, A TIT WITH "WHO BLAMYTH THIS ALE." BELOW ARE A CROWNED TUDOR ROSE WITH INITIALS OF HENRY VIII, AND THE SAME WITH A SHEAF OF ARROWS, A BADGE OF KATHARINE OF ARAGON.

FIG. 52. NUN APPLETON HALL, YORK. SUNDIAL AND FOUR
SEASONS BY H. GYLES OF YORK, 1670.

of a church.   At Exeter Cathedral, for instance, the
six windows of each choir aisle were glazed in pairs,
the designs including hawthorn, vine, oak, ivy, and
sycamore.   At Merton College Chapel, too, the fourteen
windows, seven on either side, were " paired " as far
as their foliate designs are concerned.

　　2. *Small Panels upon Grisaille.*—As already noted,
the designers soon wearied of heraldic and coloured
geometrical devices only, and reverted to the practice—
begun at Chetwode and Stanton Harcourt—of placing
small pictorial panels of various shapes upon fields of
natural grisaille.   If the windows were of large size,
the panels were placed at intervals down the lights,
being interspaced with smaller panels containing human
heads, foliage, golden lion-faces with lolling tongues,
and such-like devices.   If, as was usually the case, the
windows were of comparatively small size, one panel
was placed about halfway down each light.   The
subjects in these small panels varied according to taste.
Sometimes they consisted of single figures of apostles
or saints, the Virgin and Child being an especial favourite,
as at Harlow in Essex and St. Michael's Church, Oxford[1] ; sometimes they consisted of scenes from Scripture
history or from the lives of the saints, a particularly
elaborate series being that in the Chapter House at
York Minster, glazed early in the fourteenth century.
The scenes were simply treated, only a few figures
being introduced.   The backgrounds were coloured,
and frequently enriched by foliate diapers produced
by covering the surface with " matt " and picking
out the required design with a pointed stick.   These
panels were usually surrounded by their borders, mostly
of two or three layers only, enriched by beading and
other forms of ornamental design.   Panels containing
single figures were usually an upright oblong surmounted
by a demi-oval head, the figure itself being placed
beneath a simple cusped arch, as at Harlow.   The

───────────
[1] These St. Michael panels, four in all, dating from about 1290, are
not actually *in situ*, and have lost all their surrounding grisaille.

next step was to surmount the upright oblong form
of panel by a simple canopy, which led to the third
type, that of—

3. *Figure or Subject and Canopy Window.*—This
was by far the most popular, and at the same time the
most characteristic, of the Decorated period of glass
painting. Moreover, it paved the way for the next
period, when canopied figures were almost always
chosen for window subjects. At first these canopies,
which were identical in type with those found on contemporary tombs and brasses, were of comparatively
simple type, consisting of little more than an arch
with crocketed central gable surmounted by a pinnacle
terminating in a foliated finial, and with lesser pinnacles
rising from the supporting shafts on either side. These
canopies were sometimes drawn on white glass with
panelling, etc., indicated in " matt," as at Deerhurst
(Glos.) (Fig. 16) ; sometimes on glass of various
colours, as in the east window of Selling Church (Kent)
(Fig. 19) (about 1299–1307), or at Trumpington in
Cambridgeshire. In the former the canopies consist
of " a ruby arch coped with yellow, the pinnacles of
which canopies are green, connected about the middle
by a cross-bar of blue." [1] These figures and canopy
panels were usually placed about halfway up the lights,
the spaces above, below, and even at the sides, when
there was room, being filled with quarries or interlaced
leaded patterns, enriched in either case with foliage.
In the larger windows it was usual to break up the
lower half of the light with smaller roundels containing
human heads, or geometrical patterns placed at intervals
down the lights, as at Merton College, Oxford, or, perhaps, with a shield-of-arms, as in the choir clerestory
of Exeter Cathedral.

But the surmounting canopies soon rose to monstrous
and wholly disproportionate heights, filling (with the
panels beneath them) nearly the entire light, so that
the white pattern fields could only appear in the space

[1] Nelson, p. 127.

usually left between the base of the panel and the bottom
of the window itself.   Even this space was often partly
filled with heraldry, as in Bristol Cathedral, and Tewkesbury Abbey (see Fig.22 and p.98). These lofty canopies
were for the most part executed in white and brownish-
yellow pot-metal, " yellow stain " not making its general
appearance until comparatively late in the period.   The
design (Fig. 17) was usually a flat central part rising
just above the gable of the arch containing the figure
itself.   From this rose a lofty central tower and
spire with lesser shafts on either side of it, each surmounted by a gable and spire, the spires terminating
in elaborate finials.   The central part of the canopy
was often enriched by windows painted upon variously
coloured pieces of pot-metal, while the whole surface
(which was perfectly flat, no perspective being attempted
until much later in this period) was picked out in matt
to imitate stonework, bands of coloured glass being
introduced at intervals to represent string-courses.
The supporting side-shafts usually rose nearly as high
as those of the canopy itself, to which they were joined
at intervals by flying buttresses.

Another canopy design was that found in the west
windows of the nave aisles in York Minster.   It consisted
of three tiers of diminishing width, the lowest containing
the gable over the niche and flat platform ; the middle
with open arcading surmounted by a second crocketed
gable ;   the topmost, itself a small niche, containing a
little figure on a coloured field with gabled canopy
above.   The entire erection in this case was executed
chiefly in white enriched with yellow stain of a strong
brassy tone.   These tall canopies were usually placed
upon coloured backgrounds of green, blue, and red,
enriched by foliate diapers picked out of a " matted "
surface by the aid of a pointed stick.

Occasionally a large window was made up of two,
or even of three, rows of canopied panels.   Sometimes
these were interspaced by a shield or coloured roundel,
a second such device being set below the lower row,

and the whole placed upon quarry fields. Most of the aisle windows in the nave of York Minster were glazed in this manner. Another method was to make the topmost pinnacle of the canopies in the bottom tier support the bases, if any, of the row above, the backgrounds in this case being coloured throughout, and without intervening bands of quarry work. The great west window of York Minster, glazed in 1338, and containing three rows of canopied panels, was treated in this manner, as were the five windows in the Lady Chapel of Wells Cathedral, the latter, which are very late in date,[1] containing two rows only.

The figures of the Decorated period were tall, slim, and somewhat ungraceful, the **S** curve, noted as occurring late in the last period, having now become very much more marked, so that in some cases figures were made to appear as though in motion, when according to the nature of the subject they were really at rest. Occasionally, however, the figures stood quite upright, as in the west windows of York Minster.

Faces and all flesh tones were for the most part still painted on brown-pink pot-metal, although buff and even white glass was also used for that purpose. Features were better drawn, the faces being oval with small chins, and lips drawn separately. The eyes were large and more naturally depicted, though with a marked tendency to squint sideways. The hair, which was represented in flowing strands, was sometimes drawn on the same piece of glass as the head, sometimes leaded on separately, as in the traceries of the retro-quire windows of Wells Cathedral (e.g. see Fig. 28); or leaded on and stained yellow, as in the "Peter de Dene " window in the north nave aisle of York Minster. Occasionally red or blue glass was used to denote both

[1] [The Dean of Wells, Dr. J. Armitage Robinson, has discovered in the side windows the names of some of the donors of this glass, such as Dean Husee, who died in 1305, and Canons belonging to the beginning of the fourteenth century, and suggests that the date of the windows must be put back accordingly. See the *Graphic*, January 10, 1925 ; *Bath and Wells Diocesan Gazette*, January and December 1924, March 1925.]

hair and beards, as in the Tree of Jesse that fills the east window of the choir at Wells Cathedral. Haloes were coloured, and therefore leaded on separately. Hands and feet were still badly drawn, the fingers usually being both long and thin.

The robes of these figures were gaily coloured and simple in type. They usually consisted of a loose mantle of one colour over a tunic or gown of another, green and yellow being an especially favourite combination, though green and white, or red, green, blue, and brown-purple were also used. A mantle was sometimes lined with a second colour and even bordered with a third, as at Tewkesbury Abbey. Occasionally the under-robe was leaded up in bars of different colours in an attempt to indicate brocade, as in the choir east windows of Exeter Cathedral and Tewkesbury Abbey, or stained in bars and circles, as in a window of York Minster. In every case the colour of a robe and mantle differed from that of the background of the niche. These figures were placed within an arch, cusped either in trefoil or in cinquefoil. Above this arch was usually a high gable, outlined in colour, its front pierced with traceried openings and surmounted by foliated crockets, the whole terminating in a large foliated finial.

Occasionally, as in the great west window of York Minster, glazed in 1338 at the cost of William Melton, Archbishop of York, the niches were vaulted with ribs running to a central boss—a treatment that foreshadowed the next period (1350–1400). The backgrounds of these niches were composed of rich colours, such as blue, green, or red, usually elaborately diapered with natural foliate patterns, the trefoil, or clover leaf, being a special favourite. Another method of treating the background was to cover it with a lattice-work composed of strips of white or coloured glass, the lozenges so formed being in colour, and decorated with foliate patterns. Examples of this treatment may be seen at Eaton Bishop in Herefordshire. All shading in the Decorated period was of the " smear " type,

laid on in a wash where required, but not "worked
up" afterwards.   The shadows in the folds of draperies,
especially of large figures, were often quite deep, owing
to the quantity of pigment used, but the folds themselves
were much more flowing than in the previous style.
Faces were sometimes shaded, a light wash of smear
being brushed on as required.

Figures of saints were now often shown as holding
each his or her distinctive emblem, usually the instru-
ment of martyrdom, such as the spiked wheel and
sword of St. Catherine of Alexandria, the flaying knife
of St. Bartholomew, or the gridiron of St. Laurence.
These figures were rarely placed upon bases, a green
mound, as at Tewkesbury Abbey, or a few black and
white tiles, as in the great east window of Exeter
Cathedral, being the only foothold ; sometimes, indeed,
the figure was poised upon a strip of " brickwork," as
at Kempsey, Worcestershire.   The appearance of an
architectural base must be regarded as a sign of late
work, as at Wells.

The picture windows of this period, apart from the
" medallion " type already described, consisted of
groups of comparatively few figures, clad as already
described, and placed like the single figures on coloured
fields beneath high canopies.   The subjects were drawn
as before from Scripture history and the lives of the
saints, and were usually somewhat stiff and lifeless in
treatment.   Little or no scenery was introduced into
these picture panels, unless as accessory to the subject
depicted.   It should be added that there was as yet
no attempt at any scheme of counter-change of colours
between backgrounds and canopy fields, such as became
the practice in the next period.   Occasionally a window
contained both figures and scenes, as in the great west
window of York Minster.

4. *Figures upon Quarry Backgrounds.*—This type,
which was very uncommon in the fourteenth century,
foreshadowed the " figure upon quarry " windows
which became so popular during the fifteenth and

sixteenth centuries (see pp. 116–120). In these windows the figures were simply embedded in a background of quarries without any intervening border whatever. The quarries themselves were of the usual " Decorated " pattern, either bearing trails of running foliage or single leaves in thin " strapwork," the whole light being usually enclosed by a coloured border. Examples of this type remain at Heybridge in Essex, Credenhill in Herefordshire (Fig. 21), and Waterperry in Oxfordshire, the last named being portraits of donors. A variation of this treatment occurs in the east window of Beer Ferrers Church in Devonshire, where figures of the donor of the glass and his wife were placed upon a lattice-work of ruby, the resulting lozenges being devoid of any decoration, and the whole set within a coloured border. This glass was apparently put up about the year 1338.

5. *Jesse Windows.*—This was by far the most effective and satisfactory form of the period, the design being no longer cramped within a single lancet but spread over the six or seven lights of a large window. The general scheme was almost always the same, the details differing according to individual circumstances. Jesse himself lay on his side across the bottom of the central lights with a great vine stem rising from him, spreading outwards and upwards through the lights, and twisting into ovals or loops. Within the openings thus formed stood the several figures, both kings and prophets, the latter, who foretold Christ's coming, being placed in the side-lights. The backgrounds of these panels were often diapered and usually made to counter-change in colour with that of the field outside the surrounding vine stems. The stem itself with its branches and tendrils was usually painted on white or yellow, the leaves, copied closely from nature, being drawn on glass of various colours, whilst bunches of fruit were introduced here and there, also drawn on coloured glass. The lights were generally surrounded by coloured borders. The tracery above was filled with various

subjects, the Last Judgment being an especial favourite, as at Wells Cathedral and Selby Abbey.

Inscriptions were still executed in Lombardic characters and treated as in earlier periods, but it is important to observe that they were now both in Latin and Norman-French, the latter being at this time the language of the Court, and therefore chiefly used by the nobility. An example of an invocatory inscription worded in Norman-French remains in the great east window of St. Mary's Church, Shrewsbury, where a Tree of Jesse (not actually *in situ*) was the gift of Sir John Charlton, as recorded by the following legend, set across the bottom of the lights (Fig. 18) : " Priez p(ou)r Mons Iohan de Carleton q(ui) fist fare ceste

FIG. 18.—ST. MARY'S, SHREWSBURY.
Part of inscription for Sir John de Charlton.

verrure et p(u)r Dame Hawis sa companion."[1]   The names of saints were, however, usually in Latin and set upon labels placed at the base of the panel.   Sometimes a label bearing the name was held in the figure's hands, as in the choir clerestory of Exeter Cathedral, where St. Philip holds a scroll lettered " Philipe Apostol."

The borders were always a great feature in Decorated glass, and contained a large variety of designs.   They might consist of repeats of natural foliage, such as oak, maple, ivy, or vine leaves ; sometimes drawn in matt on white, and set on colour ; sometimes in two colours, perhaps green leaves with a brown stem set upon red

[1] Nelson, p. 180. "Pray for Sir John de Carleton [or Charlton] who caused this painted window to be made and for the Lady Hawis his companion."

or blue. Or, again, it was often the practice to draw sprays of oak or other foliage in matt on pieces of dull yellow pot-metal, and to place them as facing alternately inwards and outwards, in either case on a coloured field.

Heraldic devices were frequently used as border subjects. At Wells Cathedral the windows in the choir and Lady Chapel were bordered with gold lions on ruby fields for England, or with gold fleurs-de-lis on blue for France, an arrangement which recalls the item recorded in Chapter II, p. 21, of the purchase for Windsor Castle in 1351 from John Brampton and Henry Stathern of 1,336 feet of painted glass with borders of the King's arms. Other popular heraldic devices were the triple-towered castle of Castile (Fig. 29), usually painted on white or dull yellow pot-metal (for Eleanor of Castile, Queen of King Edward I), used as border subjects in Merton College Chapel, Oxford, and in some of the Chapter House windows at York Minster; eagles " displayed " (i.e. with expanded wings) for the Empire, with reference to Edward I's uncles, the Emperor Frederick II and Richard, King of the Romans; and covered cups or chalices, the badge of Galicia, each piece, whatever its design, being painted upon a separate piece of glass, divided from the next by a portion of coloured glass. Sometimes more than one device appeared in the same border, as in the south-east window of the Chapter House at York, where the centre light was bordered with covered cups alternating with the castles of Castile, the same devices and arrangement occurring also in a window of All Saints', North Street, of that city. Other border subjects included knights wearing heraldic surcoats over their armour, secular canons seated in their stalls, apes playing musical instruments, squirrels and falcons, all of which were used in various aisle windows in the nave of York Minster.

The tracery lights were another important feature in windows of this period, their treatment being as varied as that of the borders. The subjects included natural foliage painted upon white or greenish white, sometimes with centres of coloured bosses, as at Merton College, Oxford, and in the choir clerestories of Exeter Cathedral; foliate quarries sometimes interspaced by *coloured* strapwork, as at Tewkesbury; or large sprays of vine or ivy leaves painted upon yellow or white glass and placed upon ruby fields. Examples of the last named occur in Bristol Cathedral, Tewkesbury Abbey, and the Chapter House of Wells Cathedral. Grotesque beasts were sometimes introduced into tracery lights, drawn on coloured glass set on coloured fields within borders, while human heads or busts were of frequent occurrence. These might be placed on foliate fields drawn in matt on white, or on coloured diapers. Sometimes labels inscribed with their names were placed beneath them or across the backgrounds, the inscriptions being then so arranged as to be bisected by the head itself, as in the retro-choir of Wells Cathedral (Fig. 18). The traceries of several windows in the Lady Chapel and retro-choir of Wells Cathedral were filled in this way, as were some of the windows of Bristol Cathedral and Mottisfont Church, Hants. Figures, or even scenes, were sometimes placed in traceries, the Lord in Glory, the Virgin and Child, or the Coronation of the Virgin being of common occurrence. Saintly personages were also depicted, as in the choir aisles of Wells Cathedral, at Morpeth Church, Northumberland (Fig. 20), and in Stanford Church, Northamptonshire.

Pictorial subjects were of rare occurrence, but the east window of the south transept in Oxford Cathedral contains, among others, panels with the Martyrdom of St. Thomas of Canterbury and St. Martin dividing his Cloak with the Beggar, while at Chinnor Church in the same county the chancel traceries retain two of the Seven Works of Mercy. Figures of the Lord in Glory were frequently surrounded by the emblems of the four Evangelists : the winged man or angel for St. Matthew, the winged lion for St. Mark, a winged

ox for St. Luke, and an eagle for St. John, each usually
accompanied by a scroll inscribed with its name. Each
of these emblems typified some particular characteristic
of Christ as expounded by the individual Evangelist :
the angel (or human form) being symbolical of Christ's
human nature ; the lion, of the Resurrection, in allusion
to a mediæval belief that the young of the lion was
born dead and after some days was called into life by
its father. The ox was symbolic of sacrifice, in allusion
to the Sacrifice and the Priesthood of Christ as written
of by St. Luke ; while St. John, who took the highest
flight of all, and searched with steadfast eyes the exalted
mysteries of the Word, was represented by the eagle,
as it soared highest among birds. Angels swinging
censers or playing musical instruments were also placed
in tracery lights, being frequently twisted into extraordinary and unnatural postures in order to fit the
openings. The angels of the Decorated period were
always shown with coloured, often bi-coloured, wings,
and usually with coloured robes.

Heraldry played an ever-increasing part in window
decoration during this period. As already noted, it
was used for borders and to enrich grisaille-pattern
windows. But it was also frequently placed in the
tracery openings, as in the great east window of
Bristol Cathedral, glazed between 1312 and 1322, in
all the Chapter House windows of York Minster, and
in Upper Froyle Church in Hampshire. Another place
for shields was on the quarry fields beneath or between
the panels in a figure and canopy window. Shields
when so placed were usually surrounded by an ornamental frame, a lozenge intersecting a quatrefoil being
an especially favourite design. The space between
shield and frame was filled in with colours enriched
by foliate diapering (Fig. 22). The later shields of
the period differed from the earlier in that they were
now often " charged " with one coat-of-arms " im-
paling " another, or divided into four quarters, each
bearing one coat-of-arms. Moreover, their fields were

frequently enriched by diaper work. The Royal Arms
of England in this period changed from three golden
lions only to a shield of four quarters, two of which
contained the gold leopards on ruby as before, while
the others bore the fleurs-de-lis of France. This
change was made in 1340 consequent upon the claim
in that year of Edward III to the Crown of France.

Another feature of the Decorated period was the
appearance for the first time of figures of the donors of
windows. These figures were usually placed at the
base of the lights, attired as befitted their individual
rank in life, and represented as kneeling in prayer.
Sometimes, however, they were placed in the side-
lights of a figure and canopy window, as in Merton
College Chapel, Oxford, where twelve out of the fourteen
choir windows each contained two conventional representations of the donor, one Henry de Mamesfeld,[1]
kneeling towards the central figure of an apostle, and
holding a scroll lettered " Magister Henricus de Mamesfeld me fecit." Occasionally these figures were depicted
as holding the model of a church in token of some
donation towards the erection or rebuilding of the
edifice in which the glass was placed. Military donors
and benefactors, in common with military saints, were
represented in the armour of the period. The earlier
examples wore chain-mail strengthened at elbows and
knees with *cuir bouilli* (leather boiled in oil) plated
with steel, and over it the long silk or linen surcoat
embroidered with their armorial bearings. Such figures
were usually armed with a long heavy sword, a small
" heater "-shaped shield (resembling the outline of
the bottom of a flat-iron) being sometimes suspended
from their shoulders by its guige or strap. An example
of this early type occurred at Aldwincle in Northamptonshire. As the century progressed, armour became a
mixture of mail and plate, while the long surcoats were
slit up the side or cut away in front in order that its

[1] The Merton glass dates from early in the fourteenth century. The
donor was a Fellow of the College, Chancellor of the University in 1311,
and Dean of Lincoln in 1315.

THE DECORATED PERIOD

wearer might run or fight on foot.[1] These military
donors were occasionally represented as standing beneath
tall canopies, as at Bristol Cathedral and Tewkesbury
Abbey. Episcopal vestments differed little from earlier
examples, except that the mitres were a little taller
and of a triangular shape, being painted on white or
coloured glass according to taste. Ladies' costumes
were comparatively simple, consisting of a loose robe,
sometimes buttoned in front, over a kirtle showing at
the wrists where the tight-fitting sleeves were buttoned.
The head was covered by a white veil, a wimple being
passed over the neck and reaching to the chin.

The Decorated period was remarkable for the development of the picture window. The artists began for
the first time to ignore the mullions and to carry their
scenes over more than one light. Thus, at Bristol
Cathedral, a Martyrdom of St. Edmund filled three
lights of a window, while at Tewkesbury Abbey the
great east window of the choir was occupied with an
elaborate Last Judgment, of which the following is a
description.

The heads of the lights and the upper panels are
filled with canopies of Decorated design upon a ruby
background, with a traceried window painted on green
glass in the centre of each canopy. Beneath these
canopies the Judgment is set. The background of this
section is a beautiful blue, and in the centre light Christ
the Judge is represented seated on a rainbow, with
hands upraised and bare feet showing the Wounds.
He wears a purple mantle with a blue border and green
lining. On His right hand is the Blessed Virgin Mother
(her head lost), also seated on a rainbow and wearing
garments of the same colours. She raises her left hand
towards her Son, whilst her right hand holds and
displays her right breast—the mother's appeal. On
the left of our Lord are the remains of the figure of
an archangel, probably St. Michael, wearing a robe of

[1] For fuller details respecting mediæval armour and costumes, readers
should consult H. Druitt, *Costume on Brasses* (London, 1906).

alternate bands of green and pot-metal yellow. In
the outer south light is a group of six apostles with
St. Paul in the foreground, while the corresponding
light on the north has the remaining five apostles,
including St. Peter with the keys, and in the foreground
St. John the Baptist in a yellow mantle lined with red,
raising his left hand towards Christ. Beneath are
smaller panels with figures. In the northernmost
light, on our Lord's right hand, an angel urges forward
the saved : five nude figures, three male and two female,
among them being a mitred bishop or abbot. In the
next two lights the Resurrection of the Dead is represented. In each light an angel is flying down from
above, blowing a long trumpet, and in each panel
several persons appear rising from coffins, or from the
green earth ; and in each group is one wearing a mitre.
Others have crosses on their foreheads. These are
evidently the " dead in Christ," the sheep of Matt.
xxii. 31. In the next light an angel with red and yellow
drapery and gold wings brandishing a sword of red
flame is driving away the lost, three nude figures, two
male and one female. Around these the Devil, who is
in brown with a band of green around the neck, and
has a curious head with a beak-like nose, has cast a
chain, and is hauling them off. In the southernmost
light is a nude kneeling female figure against a background made up of horizontal diapered stripes alternately
blue and white. This represented the donor. At
the bottom of the window are armorial shields. The
great rose which forms the tracery is filled with the
Coronation of the Virgin, which is set in the centre
quatrefoil surrounded by angels censing or playing
musical instruments.[1]

In texture, the glass of the Decorated period was
still very thick and uneven, but of good quality and,

[1] The above description has been compiled from Mr. G. McN. Rushforth's article in *Transactions of the Bristol and Glos. Archæological Society*,
vol. xlvi (1924), pp. 289–324, combined with a description written by
Mr. W. G. Bannister, the verger of Tewkesbury Abbey.

generally speaking, not much affected by corrosion. The blues become softer in tone. Most of the white glass had a marked greenish tone, a notable exception being the early geometrical grisaille in Exeter Cathedral (see p. 79), which was of an extraordinarily pure white tone.

By this time yellow stain had been discovered, possibly as early as 1306. But its adoption was certainly not general, and it cannot be said to have played a great part in the Decorated period. It was used freely in the nave and Chapter House windows of York Minster; in such profusion, indeed, as to suggest that the York glass painters were the first to make the discovery, though its strong brassy tone shows that they were not fully acquainted with its properties. It was only sparingly used in Bristol Cathedral and Tewkesbury Abbey, and not at all in the choir of Exeter Cathedral (glazed between 1300 and 1320), nor in Merton College Chapel, glazed about 1310.

About 1340 it began to be much better known, and its general use gradually brought about the change into the next style of glass painting. It was used freely in the choir and Lady Chapel of Wells Cathedral, where the glass may be as late as 1345.[1] This glass certainly showed marked signs of the coming change to the Transition, for white glass was used in much greater proportions, and the figures were made to stand upon bases, some decorated with foliated work, others taller of a hexagonal type. In the Lady Chapel, animals such as lions were introduced into the bottom of some of the lights, being made to crouch by the bases. Both figures and canopies were placed upon coloured fields, which in the choir clerestory at least were arranged in an elementary scheme of counter-change, while in the Lady Chapel the upper tier of bases rested upon the topmost pinnacles of the lower row of canopies. In short, this Wells glass may be fitly termed the link between the two halves of the fourteenth century.

[1] [See note above, p. 84.]

CHAPTER IX

TRANSITION FROM DECORATED TO PERPEN-DICULAR (1350–1400)

As noted at the end of the last chapter, glass-painting was now undergoing considerable changes in style, due very largely to the increasing use of yellow stain, coupled with the fact that it showed to best advantage upon white glass. This in turn naturally resulted in a greater use of white glass, not only for canopy work, but also for faces and draperies, all of which could be treated with stain as required. It is possible that the general adoption of yellow stain was due in some degree to the large number of glass painters who had been summoned to Westminster from various parts of England during the years 1350–2 in order that they might work upon the glazing of King Edward III's new Chapel of St. Stephen, Westminster, and also upon that intended for St. George's Chapel at Windsor.[1] Yellow stain was certainly used in both series of windows, as fragments found in 1800 clearly showed ; moreover, the Fabric Rolls record payments for " silver filings " among the materials purchased for the use of the glaziers, which filings could only have been wanted for the purpose of making " stain." It is obvious that, if not already generally known, its properties and possibilities would soon have become clear to these experienced craftsmen, and that upon their return to their own places of business they would naturally adopt this new method of enriching their glass paintings. It was certainly a vast improvement upon pot-metal, for instead of laboriously chipping and shaping a piece

[1] This was the older Chapel of St. George, which, becoming ruinous, was replaced by the present building late in the fifteenth century.

96

of dull yellow glass when required for, say, a mitre or a crown, the designer could now if he wished first indicate with tracing pigment the outline of a head with hair, halo, and even headgear, all upon the same piece of white glass, and then float on yellow stain where required, afterwards "firing" the glass in the usual manner, while it was invaluable for purposes of enriching draperies or canopy work. It should be noted that until late in the century, say about 1380, yellow stain was still apt to be very "brassy" in tone ; also that now and during the fifteenth century it was almost invariably laid on very carefully, so as not to exceed the lines marked out for it by the tracing pigment.

In the earlier years of this Transitional period, the greater part of the work executed might fairly be described as "Decorated" in style and "Perpendicular" in execution. This was particularly the case with the great east window of Gloucester Cathedral, which is so remarkable as to deserve special notice. A vast expanse of glass measuring 78 feet in height by 38 in width, it seems to have been put up to commemorate the Battle of Crecy, fought August 26, 1346. One might indeed be pardoned for dating both this glass and the window in which it was placed as late as 1370, for the colour-scheme is purely Perpendicular in feeling, ruby, blue, white, and stain, together with a very little green and amber, being the only colours used, while the stone work itself was a mere grid, almost devoid of tracery. But examination of the heraldry displayed in its lower lights has led practically every expert to the same conclusion, namely, that the glass was in place by 1349.[1] The subject of the window was the Coronation of the Virgin Mary by her Son, attended by apostles, saints, and angels,

[1] See *Archæological Journal*, vol. xx, for a paper by C. Winston, reprinted in his *Memoirs of Glass Painting*, p. 285 ; *Transactions of the Bristol and Glos. Archæological Society*, vol. xxxviii (1916), pp. 69–97, by T. D. Grimké-Drayton. Mr. N. H. J. Westlake, F.S.A. (*History of Design in Painted Glass*, vol. ii), however, dated the glass as late as 1360, an opinion also expressed by Mr. J. A. Knowles, who points out that in 1349

together with the founders and most prominent repre-
sentatives of the Abbey of Gloucester.[1] The figures
were painted upon white glass, their draperies being
enriched by stained borders. Their haloes were coloured,
and leaded in separately, They stand upon bases
beneath canopies with groined vaults, being so arranged
that the tall crocketed central spire of the lower row
supports the pedestals of the row above it, an arrangement perhaps inspired by or copied from the glass in
the Lady Chapel of Wells Cathedral. The figures
themselves were originally arranged in pairs to face one
another, the fields of the lights being alternately ruby
and blue, with the exception of the two central lights,
which were both ruby—an arrangement of counter-
change not generally adopted until about 1380. The
backgrounds of the lights immediately to left and right
of the central pair were enriched by an elaborate
foliated pattern ; the rest, with the exception of that
containing Christ, were of plain ruby and blue. The
first three tiers from the bottom of the window were
filled with quarries, each decorated not by the usual
trailed foliage, but with a single star, the topmost row
being further enriched by a series of ornamental panels
containing shields-of-arms placed one in each light.
These three tiers only were bordered by a running
repeat of dog-roses in white and yellow and ruby.

But this window was quite exceptional in treatment
and far in advance of its period, most of the work
produced between 1350 and 1380 being still largely
Decorated in feeling, though showing a marked tendency
to improvement. The coming changes in style were
clearly indicated by the increasing use of white for
draperies, often enriched by ornamental borders, or
by powderings of foliate devices, or by bars, all executed

the Black Death had just died down, and all England was in chaos.
Mr. Knowles's paper, " The Black Death and its Effects on the Art of
Glass Painting," will be found in the *Archæological Journal*, vol. lxxix
(1922).

[1] *Transactions of the Bristol and Glos. Archæological Society*, vol.
xliv (1922), pp. 293–304, by G. McN. Rushforth, F.S.A.

in " matt " and stain. Examples of this treatment
remain in Chelsea Old Church, at Bexhill in Sussex,
and at Thornhill in the West Riding of Yorkshire, the
last named in a simple " figure on quarry " window.
Colours were, however, still frequently used for draperies,
sometimes with white mantles over them, as in the
Latin Chapel of Oxford Cathedral. Faces and flesh
tones were now frequently painted on *white* glass, the
features being more naturally drawn, while the hair
was sometimes indicated by stain. Haloes were still
usually coloured ; occasionally they were drawn in
matt and stain and then leaded in, as in an episcopal
figure in a window of Bexhill Church, Sussex ; or,
again, both head and halo were drawn on a single
piece of glass, as in a window of the Latin Chapel,
Oxford Cathedral, glazed with two others between
1367 and 1369 (Fig. 23). The **S** curve was still
retained, but became less marked as the century
progressed. Backgrounds were still for the most part
foliate in treatment, being occasionally leaded up in
alternate bars of colour and stained patterns on white,
as in a window of Tryddyn Church (Flint). The canopy
work was of decidedly Transitional type, being no longer
flat but three-sided, showing that the designers had
acquired some knowledge of perspective. They were
still executed in white glass, the various string-courses,
crockets, etc., being indicated in matt and stain. The
little traceried windows were also retained as canopy
decorations, being sometimes painted on colour but
more often on white, when they were given deep em-
brasures and white traceries picked out of black fields.
The high-pitched gables over the niches were gradually
reduced to little more than crocketed arches, cusped
in cinquefoil and surmounted by a central pinnacle,
while the supporting shafts, which were decorated in
various ways, were sometimes drawn as though set
edgeways, thus receding in perspective. The shading
used was generally " smear," laid on with a brush as
required, but not worked up as in the later part of the

century. Quarry backgrounds when used sometimes bore trailing foliage, sometimes a single leaf on each quarry, but the upper edges of each piece of glass were now generally enriched by stain, or by matt and stained borders, as in the Latin Chapel of Oxford Cathedral, an excellent example of early Transitional work. Foliated borders of the lights still occurred, usually executed in white and stain on colour; sometimes, however, they consisted of various heraldic and other designs, such as animals, birds, and lion faces set in alternation, each drawn on a separate piece of glass and interspaced by pieces of colour.

The tracery subjects were much the same as those of the Decorated period, but, like those in the main lights, contained a greater proportion of matt and stain. At Kingsdown in Kent, for instance, one tracery light was filled with a Virgin and Child set on yellow quarries, each charged with a rosette, the whole within a border of four-petalled flowers interspaced by cross-hatchings. The Virgin herself was robed in brown over green, her head with crown, wimple, and part of the Child's arm, being all drawn on the same piece of glass. Inscriptions were still executed in Lombardic characters, occasionally drawn in black outline on white. The change to " black-letter " came about 1380. Figures of donors when introduced were still placed at the foot of the lights.

It is most important to remember that though all these points should be looked for, they did not all occur in any given window of the period, as some designers were much more advanced in their ideas than others. Also it should be noted that practically every window of the period contained figures only, either under canopies or set on quarry fields. During this period (1350–80) architecture itself was going through a steady evolution towards the Perpendicular style, until by 1380 windows were being made of tall lights divided by mullions running up to the arch, the upper part subdivided into small upright lights with possibly a quatrefoil at the apex of each subdivision, thus forming the traceries, while the main lights themselves were, if the window was of any size, crossed at intervals by stone transoms dividing them into halves, thirds, or even smaller sections, thus creating several tiers of lights, each panel usually terminating in a cinquefoil head. The result of these architectural changes was that the last twenty years of the fourteenth century saw the intro- duction of the style which was to influence English glass painting for the next centuries, namely, the Perpendicular as it is generally termed, though many Decorated features lingered in it until quite the end of the century.

Figures were now taller and more graceful, though still retaining traces of the **S** curve, their faces and flesh tones being usually painted upon white glass, but occasionally upon pale pink pot-metals, as in one or two examples at New College, Oxford. Hair and beards were now stained, but frequently leaded in, in other cases they were stained on the same piece of glass as the head. Features were much more carefully drawn, the eyes being correctly delineated with iris, pupil, and eyelid, the eyebrows being somewhat arched, while nose and lips were naturally drawn. Haloes were still usually coloured, but in a few cases were drawn on the same piece of glass as the head of the figure and enriched with stained borders, as in the east window of Exeter Cathedral, enlarged and partly reglazed in 1389 by the firm of Robert Lyen.[1]

Robes were now slightly looser, and often very richly coloured; indeed, in this period the most gorgeous hues of ruby, blue, scarlet, maroon, emerald-green, olive-green, crimson, and purple were used without stint, not only for robes but also for haloes, shoes, and even for canopy vaults, as in New College ante-chapel, Oxford (glazed between 1379 and 1386 by the firm of Thomas Glazier of that city), while in the east window of Exeter Cathedral a figure of St. Catherine was robed in a ruby mantle adorned with golden lions in an attempt to indicate royal rank. White glass (which was still

[1] Bishop and Prideaux, *The Building of Exeter Cathedral*, pp. 151-4.

of a strong greenish tone) was often used for draperies
and ecclesiastical vestments, usually enriched by powderings of elaborate foliate and other devices, lattice-work
patterns, or even with the emblem of the particular
saint represented, all these devices being drawn in
matt and stain, the latter generally, though not invariably, of a much paler hue.   Such figures now usually
stood upon bases of various designs, their floors enriched
with tiled pavements, either coloured or black and
white, and of many different patterns.   Occasionally,
however, there was no room for a base, as in the great
west window of Winchester Cathedral glazed about the
year 1380.

The canopy work of this period showed abundant
signs of the coming change to pure Perpendicular.
Although usually still as lofty as that of the Decorated
period, it was now invariably composed of white glass
profusely enriched with stain, while in design the
canopies were much more open, especially in the upper
part, which was divided and subdivided into numerous
turrets and pinnacles, decorated perhaps with wind-
vanes or pennons, or surmounted by gold lions or birds.
The little traceried windows, both pot-metal and
black and white, were still retained (Fig. 24).   The
fantastic embattled turrets which were such a feature
of this period, being found at New College, Oxford, in
a window of the Lady Chapel of York Minster, and in
the south transept of Canterbury Cathedral, were
decidedly un-English in feeling, and seem to have
been copied from or inspired by very similar work in
a window of Altenberg Church in Germany.[1]   As
already noted (p. 7), much of the raw unpainted glass
used by English craftsmen was of German origin, and
it was not surprising therefore that foreign ideas as
well as foreign materials should find their way into
English glass shops.

The high-pitched gables of the Decorated period

[1] *Journal of the British Archæological Association*, October 1923:
" The York School of Glass Painting," by J. A. Knowles, p. 120.

now disappeared, although the niches below were still surmounted by crocketed arches, cusped in cinquefoil or even in sexfoil, and profusely enriched with stain. The ribbed vaults were also retained, especially by the Oxford designers. These canopies were supported upon shafts of greenish-white glass, decorated by clusters of pinnacles, lancet windows, crocketed panelling, and other devices, all drawn in matt and stain, while perspective was attempted both in canopies and bases. The shading of this period was of the type known as " smear shading stippled," that is, the pigment was first laid on in a wash where required and then worked up by dabbing it with a brush. The elaborately diapered foliated backgrounds gradually gave place to a sort of foliage or " seaweed " pattern with jagged edges, whilst the backgrounds of the canopies and those of the base began to be arranged in a scheme of counterchange, ruby with blue and vice versa, with those of the niche fields set between them, and again with those on either side. Foliate borders fell into disuse, the niche with its canopy shafts either extending to the edge of the stonework or being separated from it by a thin strip of white glass.

Picture windows were not popular in this period, but the great west window of Winchester Cathedral seems to have been partly glazed in this manner, for it contained at least twelve scenes from the life of Christ, each occupying a single light beneath a canopy, the side-lights being filled by canopied figures of apostles and prophets.[1]

The Jesse window of this period was merely an improvement upon that of the Decorated period, the chief difference being that the backgrounds of lights and sometimes of alternate panels were usually made to counter-change red with blue. The stem was naturally drawn with knots and tendrils, the fruit and foliage being coloured, while the robes of the various

---

[1] This window was overhauled and partially releaded in 1921 under the writer's direction, when the original scheme was discovered.

kings and prophets were richly coloured, the figures
themselves being identified by their names inscribed
upon short scrolls (Figs. 47, 48, and p.152). The tracery
was usually occupied by the Last Judgment.

All inscriptions were now in " black-letter," drawn
in black on white glass. Dedicatory inscriptions were
now in Latin only, which with the contractions used
often made them difficult to decipher. Thus the side-
windows of Winchester College Chapel each bore the
legend (Fig. 25) : " Orate p̄ Willmō de Wykehā |
epō Wyntōn ffundatore | istius Collegii " [1] (" Pray for
William of Wykeham, Bishop of Winchester, founder

FIG. 25.   ONE OF WILLIAM OF WYKEHAM'S INSCRIPTIONS IN WINCHESTER
COLLEGE CHAPEL.

of this College "). In the case of saintly personages
their titles were usually placed on the fronts of their
bases : Scs (Sanctus) for a male saint, such as Scs
Nicholas, or Sca (Sancta) for a female saint, Sca Anna,
St. Anne. Figures of prophets were distinguished by
the contraction " pph." or " ppha." (for propheta)
placed *after* their names, such as " Amos pph." or
" Malachias ppha." Figures of apostles and prophets
were sometimes shown as holding long twisted scrolls
inscribed with Creed sentences, or with corresponding
sentences from the Old Testament respectively, such
inscriptions being frequently " contracted " and other-

[1] This inscription if fully extended would read: " Orate p(ro) Will-
(el)mo de Wykeha(m) Ep(iscop)o Wynton(iensi) ffundatore istius Col-
legii." The brackets indicate the portions omitted.

wise incomplete, as at New College and in the great west window of Winchester Cathedral.

Tracery lights were now filled with small figures of saints or angels, the latter including the Celestial Hierarchies (as at New College), or with such subjects as the Coronation of Mary. These figures were chiefly drawn in matt and stain on white, and were sometimes set beneath diminutive canopies, their backgrounds counter-changing blue with red, as in the main lights, sometimes upon coloured fields within ornamental borders, as in a window of Wimbledon Church, Surrey. The smaller openings, such as quatrefoils, octofoils, and small triangular spandrels might contain foliage, lion faces, or monsters.

Angelic figures (other than those of the Nine Orders), both of this and of the next period, were divided into two distinct types : those vested in white albs or robes, and those whose bodies, arms, and legs were covered by golden feathers. The latter treatment was clearly inspired by the miracle plays, in which persons taking the part of angels usually wore feathered tights. In either case their wings were of gold, and no longer bi-coloured, while the feathered angels were often equipped with six wings and poised on golden wheels, the emblem of swiftness.[1] It was in this period, too, that angels were first represented as holding shields, fragments of an angelic figure treated in this manner remaining at the top of the great west window of Winchester Cathedral. Heraldry, when it occurred, was displayed upon shields of a somewhat lengthened " heater " shape, sometimes enriched by natural foliate diapers. The charges were, however, still comparatively simple, consisting at most of four quarterings. The practice of " abrading " or filing away the " flash" of ruby glass and staining the exposed white surface was also first introduced in this period, an example occurring in a shield with the arms of William of Wykeham— argent (white) two chevrons sable (black) between three

[1] Ezek. x. 9.

roses gules (red)—in a staircase window at New College, Oxford. The yellow centres of the red roses were obtained by the process of "abrasion and staining."

Figures of donors and benefactors were usually placed at the foot of a window, more rarely in the tracery lights, being depicted as kneeling in prayer, sometimes to the figure of a saint or even to the vision of some scriptural incident, as in the east window of Winchester College Chapel,[1] where the founder, William of Wykeham (see above), kneels before the Annunciation.

The armour of this period, as worn by saints or donors of military rank, consisted of a chain-mail shirt or hauberk; over it first a cuirass of steel, and then a leather jupon or close-fitting tunic without sleeves and finished with a scalloped edge. The arms and legs were encased in plate, the hands being covered by flexible gauntlets and the feet by pointed "sollerets." The head was covered by a conical "bascinet," to which was laced a chain camail or tippet covering neck and shoulders. The weapons carried were usually a long heavy sword suspended by a belt of golden plates round the hips, and a spear. Regal figures, whether saintly or not, wore a long tunic, frequently decorated with stained patterns; in white over it, a long loose mantle, the shoulders being covered by an ermine tippet. The regal crown of the period was tall with rich foliate ornaments rising from the rim. Bishops were usually vested in the chasuble over dalmatic and alb, their mitres being taller than before, and of a conical type, drawn in matt and stain. The black habit of Benedictine saints was usually represented by deep blue (see Chapter V, p. 46). Civilian figures wore long plain gowns with tight sleeves and a hood, the men having short forked beards and close-cut hair, while ladies wore a long plain robe cut square at the neck and buttoned down the front, with an

[1] This glass was replaced by a modern copy in 1822 (see Chapter XV, p. 165).

under-garment showing at the wrists. Their hair was plaited and gathered into a net.

In texture the glass of this period varied considerably, the white being still of a strong greenish tone, and often very thick and uneven. In quality it was often exceedingly poor and greatly corroded, the rubies and blues being frequently so opaque that the designs painted on them were practically invisible. This deterioration was probably due to the mortality caused by the Black Death of 1348–9, which in many places left only raw apprentices and labourers to carry on the work of glass making.

CHAPTER X

PERPENDICULAR (1400–1500)

WITH the fifteenth century and the full establishment of the Perpendicular style of architecture, with its enormous increase of window-space coupled with a simpler form of tracery, came a corresponding increase in the demand for coloured glass which, so far as English work was concerned, may be said to have reached its highest point of development about 1485. It was indeed a century of building and of rebuilding. On all sides stately churches were rising, and great cathedrals, abbeys, and priories were being rebuilt in the Perpendicular style or their windows enlarged in order to receive as much painted glass as possible. Indeed, many churches of this period may be described as veritable " lanterns of glass," so narrow was the wall-space left between their great windows.

It should be added that the outbreak in 1460 of the " Wars of the Roses " was not a war of the people, and indeed made but little difference to them. It was essentially a war of the nobility and their retainers ; and though both Yorkists and Lancastrians used on occasion to issue Commissions of Array to call out the Shire-levies (Militia), yet not one single town " chose to stand a siege during the whole war ; whatever the temper of the citizens, they used to open their gates to any leader who appeared before them with a sufficient force." [1]   Neither can it be said that the belligerents interfered to any great extent with the daily life of the people, so that, as the result of this mutual neutrality, the progress of fine art in all its forms was allowed to continue unchecked.

[1] *Mediæval England*, p. 139.

As far as glass painting was concerned, the style pursued was that gradually evolved during the second half of the preceding century, which had by now lost practically all traces of Decorated feeling.

The glass painters now began to put their painting first and their glazing second—that is to say, they used larger pieces of glass to build up their panels, the lead-lines no longer playing the most prominent part in determining outlines, while the colours used, although much less varied in hue, were far more brilliant and sparkling, so that the painted windows of this century have been likened to " spacious seas of silver washed with blue and gold."

All windows of this period may for convenience be divided into four distinct types, each of which, though agreeing in general technique one with the other, yet possessed its own peculiar characteristics. The types were :

1. Figure and canopy windows.
2. Subject windows.
3. Quarry windows.
4. Jesse windows.

1. *Figure and Canopy Windows.*—These were very popular all through the century. The figures were tall and graceful, and much better proportioned, while all traces of the **S** curve disappeared. The hands were more correctly drawn, while the feet were smaller and not so prominently exhibited. The anatomy of nude figures, too, was much better, though the feet were often disproportionately large. Faces with hair, halo, and headgear were almost invariably painted upon one piece (or at most two or three pieces leaded together) of white glass, the stain being introduced where needed ; the haloes especially being usually decorated by an ornamental yellow border. Occasionally, however, pale pink pot-metal was used for faces, as in a small figure of a St. Christopher in a window of St. Thomas's Church, Salisbury. Colour, too, was sometimes used for haloes, as in the Beauchamp

Chapel, Warwick, glazed in 1447 by John Prudde of Westminster (see page 19), at West Wickham and at Thannington in Kent, both these being of late fifteenth-century date. The treatment of the features became much more refined and often quite beautiful, the faces being oval with highly arched eyebrows, and eyes, nose, and mouth were all carefully drawn. Hair was usually stained ; sometimes it was merely grey, but the leaded-on coloured hair of the previous century fell into complete disuse. The shading both of faces and robes varied considerably. In the earlier years of the century it was still of the type termed " smear shaded stipple " : during the middle of the century pure " stipple " was used, that is, a slight wash was laid on all over the glass and worked up as required, although in small figures or heads hardly any shading at all was apparent, as in the case of a small St. Margaret at Herriard Church, Hants. As the century advanced, the shading became more and more pronounced, until by 1490 it was often quite heavy and dense, hair and beards being worked out into long curls, and faces and draperies deeply shaded.

The robes worn by these figures were also looser, with large folds indicated by means of shading, or sometimes by leadlines, as at Cirencester in Gloucestershire. The rich and varied colours used during the Transition period both for draperies and backgrounds fell into disuse, possibly owing to their costliness, the chief colours now being ruby, blue (often of a marked purplish tone), green, and maroon, with, of course, white and yellow stain. The last-named varied somewhat in tone, but was always carefully laid on so as to keep within the lines prepared for it. The robes of saintly personages usually consisted of a mantle of one colour over a garment of another, the colours being invariably arranged so as to counter-change with those of the background. A common scheme was a white mantle decorated, or perhaps merely bordered, with matt and yellow stain, over red or blue ; but colour over colour was also frequently employed, the borders of

matt and stain being then leaded on, as in the east
window of Fromond's Chantry in Winchester College
and of Ross Church, Herefordshire. Another method
of decorating borders, and sometimes the robes themselves, was to drill holes in the glass and to insert
therein pieces of coloured glass of various shapes,
square, round, lozenge, or oval, one piece in each hole,
thus producing the effect of a jewelled border. Occasionally haloes were treated in this manner, as
at Browne's Hospital at Stamford in Lincolnshire.
This practice, however, did not come into fashion
until about the middle of the fifteenth century, and
was never universally popular, owing to the labour
entailed and the consequent costliness. Good examples
of robes or borders of robes treated in this manner
remain in the Beauchamp Chapel, Warwick (Fig.
33), Ludlow Church (Salop), and Nettlestead Church
(Kent). Royal saints such as St. Edward the
Confessor, or St. Edmund the Martyr, usually wore
a long mantle lined with ermine, and ermine tippet,
over a tunic; while military saints were clad in the
armour of the period (see p. 127), sometimes with coloured
mantles over, as in the east window of the Lady Chapel
of Gloucester Cathedral. Ecclesiastical saints, whether
archbishops, bishops, or deacons, usually wore Mass
vestments, consisting of chasuble over dalmatic, tunicle,
and alb, or in the case of a deacon, dalmatic only
over alb. Archbishops were distinguished not only
by the cross staff that they carried in place of the
crozier, but by the pallium, a strip of white lamb's-wool
enriched with cross-headed pins, worn over the chasuble.
The cope, a processional vestment, was sometimes
worn by episcopal saints.

Wavy scrolls were frequently introduced into these
figure windows, sometimes held, sometimes suspended
as it were in the air over a figure's head. They might
bear Creed sentences if for an apostle, Old Testament
sentences for a prophet, or perhaps clauses of the Te
Deum, or even the name only of the person represented,

as in a window of Morley Church, Derbyshire. These
inscriptions were in Latin, and set out in "black-
letter." The figures, whatever their rank, usually
stood upon bases of various designs, all drawn in matt
and stain upon white glass, their fronts being three-
sided, or with flanking wings, while their floors were
decorated with tiled pavements of very many patterns,
executed in black, white, gold, and brown, and occasionally in colour. Sometimes the back edge of the
pavement was enriched by a low gold cresting, as in
the east window of Fromond's Chantry in Winchester
College, and in Little Malvern Priory Church.

The surmounting canopies or "tabernacles," as they
were sometimes called, were now of very many types,
their design largely depending upon the taste of the
individual glass painter. In general principle of construction, however, they were nearly always the same,
being drawn on white glass enriched with stain where
required, and decorated with numerous little crocketed
pinnacles, spirelets, and turrets, which sometimes
bore wind-vanes, pennons, or even square banners
(Fig. 26). In other cases some of the pinnacles
were flat-topped and surmounted by gold lions or eagles.
Little half-figures of angels, robed in white and with
gold hair, were often used as canopy decorations, being
framed in small openings with coloured backgrounds,
or peeping round the corner of a pinnacle base. Occasionally, too, the front of a canopy itself was pierced
to accommodate a shield charged with heraldry, as
at Almondbury in Yorkshire (Fig. 27) and at St. Peter's
Church, Canterbury.

Another late-fifteenth-century type of canopy had a
three-sided front enriched with inserted "jewels," and
surmounted by cresting. Above this might be a lesser
story of open arcading supporting a golden roof adorned
with pinnacles, as at Little Malvern and in Fromond's
Chantry Chapel, Winchester College. Sometimes the
crested front was surmounted by a tent-like dome, as in
the east window of Buckland Church, Gloucestershire.

The vaults within were sometimes groined in matt and stain, and supported on rear columns partly hidden by the figure. More often the front of the niche only was vaulted, being frequently divided into a series of arcades each with its own vault, divided one from the other by foliated pendants.

These canopies were usually carried upon shafts of white enriched with stain and decorated at intervals with clusters of pinnacles, or panelling surmounted by crocketed gables, or with mouldings filled with "ball-flower." A form of decoration very popular with the York designers was the introduction about halfway down in the shafts of a small human figure, itself set on a base beneath a little canopy (Fig. 29). This idea, which occurred also in some of the nave clerestory windows of Winchester Cathedral (glazed early in the fifteenth century probably by the firm of Thomas of Oxford), seems to have been of foreign origin, as it appears also in the famous "Braunche" brass in St. Margaret's Church, King's Lynn, which is Flemish or German work of mid-fourteenth-century date.[1] A slight variation of the idea occurred at All Souls' College and in the choir clerestories of Winchester Cathedral, where the niches, which were much smaller and adorned with tiled pavements and groined vaults, were filled with crouching gold lions.

These canopied figures were placed against coloured backgrounds so arranged as to counter-change both with their robes and with the backgrounds of the canopy and base, the next lights on either side alternating again. An exception might be made if the figures depicted the Nine Orders of Angels, as at Great Malvern, where all seven of a set of nine (two now lost) are set upon blue diapered with conventional clouds, to show that they belong to heaven. The most usual colours employed for niche backgrounds were ruby and blue, but both green and maroon were also used, as were white and stain, stain only, or even white only. The diapers

[1] Macklin, *The Brasses of England* (The Antiquary's Books, 1907), p. 92.

were many and varied, by far the most popular being
the monotonous " seaweed " pattern which had replaced
natural foliate designs about 1380.   Closely set rosettes
were also frequently employed.   Another type used
at Cirencester consisted of a large pattern of pomegranates in white and stain, while other types included
damask patterns in black outline on green, or gold,
or white and gold.

Occasionally some attempt was made to introduce
scenery into these figure panels, especially in those
representing the giant St. Christopher (see Fig.
34). At Malvern, for instance, this saint is shown
as picking his way through a stream with little trees
and plants on either side of its banks, all placed
on his base instead of tiles ; while in a St. Christopher
window at Thaxted in Essex quite a pretty little picture
was introduced, including a mill with water-wheel,
a small ship under sail, and a sea-monster, the river-
bank being decked with trees and foliage, the whole
executed in matt and stain on white glass.

2. *Subject Windows.*—These became exceedingly
popular during the fifteenth century, the subjects
depicted being many and varied (see Chapter V).
These windows were usually filled with small panels
arranged in rows across the lights, the series generally
beginning at the top left-hand corner. Each row
was set beneath canopies, those below the top row
consisting of little more than arches, sometimes enriched with yellow vaulting, while their backgrounds
were alternately blue and red.

Towards the middle of the fifteenth century pictures
became larger, each panel occupying one light, as in
the " St. Werstan " window at Malvern, or the " Pal-
mer's " window at Ludlow (Fig. 30), or were made
to extend over two or more lights. A Crucifixion
scene, for example, was usually made to occupy three
lights, Christ being in the centre with St. Mary and St.
John on either side, while an Annunciation might fill two
lights, the Virgin with her desk and lily-pot being in

one, and in the other the Archangel Gabriel with his
virge or rod of office (not a sceptre) and scroll inscribed : " Ave Maria gratia plena, Dominus tecum." [1]
The pictures in these windows were as a rule clearly
expressed, containing comparatively few figures, while
the scenery and all accessory details were generally of
a simple nature, due no doubt to the influence exercised
by the miracle plays, whence the artists must have
obtained many of their ideas. Thus an ecclesiastical
or domestic interior would be indicated by little more
than a tapestried background pierced by a window
or a door, and with an altar or a font in the foreground
if required ; while an outdoor scene was denoted by
trees, grass, and rocks, drawn in colour or in matt
and stain, with perhaps the gable end of a " house "
at one side, or a tower or two in the distance.

As a rule, though not invariably, these pictorial
panels, when arranged in rows, were divided horizontally,
one from another, by " labels " or bands of white glass
bearing explanatory " black-letter " inscriptions, one
beneath each picture (Fig. 31). These sentences were
usually in Latin, often beginning with the word
" Hic " (here), such as, " Hic Deus designat mundum "
(" Here God plans the world "), which explained the
first panel of a Creation series at St. Neot in Cornwall.
Sometimes, however, English was used for this purpose,
as in a window at Morley Church, Derbyshire. Occasionally lettered scrolls were introduced into the picture
itself, as at Clavering in Essex (Fig. 32), where
in a panel depicting St. Catherine disputing with the
Philosophers, a scroll lettered " Credo in Deum Patrem "
(" I believe in God the Father ") was made to issue
from her mouth, to which one philosopher replied
" Ego probo " (" I approve "), and a second " Ego
nego " (" I deny ").[2] The colour-scheme of this panel
is as follows : " St. Catherine, in a blue mantle and gold

---

[1] " Hail, Mary, full of grace, the Lord is with thee."
[2] The legend is that the Emperor Maxentius sent fifty learned doctors
and philosophers to reason with St. Catherine, but that instead she con-
verted them all to Christianity, whereupon all fifty were put to death

crown, is standing on the left, with her hands raised, addressing the philosophers, who are seated more or less in a ring in the middle of the picture. Four out of the fifty philosophers are here shown, dressed in red and blue gowns and hoods, two of them with round caps, one with the tonsure. . . . The king, who has a white beard, is enthroned on the right; he wears a rich crown, has a white coat, and over it a cloth-of-gold mantle, trimmed with yellow fur, with a fur cape. The oak-leaf background of the whole scene is murrey-coloured." [1]

During the second half of the fifteenth century there was a growing tendency upon the part of designers to dispense with the surmounting canopy both in figure- and subject-windows, and either to carry the picture or its background right up into the cusped head of the lights, as at Hillesden (Bucks) and Ludlow (Fig. 34), or to surmount it with a demi-figure of the Almighty, or of an angel issuing from conventional clouds, as in the great north window of Canterbury Cathedral. In the east window of Gloucester Cathedral Lady Chapel, glazed about 1490, the scheme seems to have been one of canopied figures alternating with scenes without canopies. [2] This treatment, again, was either derived from continental sources or was actually the work of foreign glass painters, several of whom were resident in England about this period; for, as will be seen (see Chapter XI), it was a marked feature of Flemish work during the next period of glass painting.

3. *Quarry Windows.*—These, too, were exceedingly popular in the fifteenth century, probably by reason of their cheapness as compared with the more elaborate canopy work. In these windows the figures, usually those of popular saints, were placed upon tiled bases,

by the Emperor's command. Another panel at Clavering shows their martyrdom by fire.

[1] See the description of the Clavering glass by Mr. F. C. Eeles in *Transactions of the Essex Arch. Society*, xvi, pt. 2.

[2] *Transactions of the Bristol and Glos. Archæological Society*, vol. xliii (1921), p. 194.

sometimes with crocketed pendants, the space above, below, and around, being filled in with lozenge-shaped quarries, the whole within coloured borders. A shield-of-arms was sometimes inserted above or below the figure with the intention of breaking up the light a little more. Sometimes a base was not provided, the figure being then suspended as it were in mid-air, as at North Cerney Church, Gloucestershire. In a few cases, notably that of St. Christopher, a stream or pool of water, perhaps containing fish, took the place of tiles upon the base-floor (Fig. 34).

Sometimes a quarry light had only a shield-of-arms, its position varying according to taste. It might be embedded in the quarries, as in the east window of the Lady Chapel in Canterbury Cathedral, or it might be set on a coloured field and surrounded by a border of twisted stems throwing out sprays of stained foliage or flowers at intervals, as at Bramley, and St. Cross' Hospital in Hampshire, and Himbleton in Worcestershire. Another treatment, which only occurred in a few churches, notably at Bledington in Gloucestershire, and Holt and Grimley in Worcestershire, was to place figures or simple scenes against damasked backgrounds of white and gold with coloured borders, the whole set upon quarry fields.

The quarries in these windows differed in treatment from those of the previous styles in that each row bore a separate device, such as conventional foliage, sprays of flowers or plants, radiant suns, monograms, and stars, all drawn in matt and stain only. Occasionally these quarries were bordered on two sides, as in earlier examples. Heraldic badges or rebuses were sometimes employed as quarry subjects, the latter being a pictorial punning device intended to represent a person's name, or perhaps surname. Such is the letter " K " and a bell for the Cable family in ancient glass in Frome Church (Somerset), or the hart lying in water, the rebus of Walter Lyhart, a fifteenth-century Bishop of Norwich, which appeared in several East Anglian churches.

Such windows were bordered with various devices, one light as a rule containing a single pattern, drawn in matt and stain on oblongs of greenish-white glass, interspaced by slips of coloured glass, chiefly red and blue. The designs were very varied, the most popular being crowns, crowned letters, blocks of conventional foliage, stained fleurs-de-lys within white foliage, heraldic devices such as the hart's head in a window of Himbleton Church, Worcestershire, or occasionally Yorkist suns, as in windows at Bramley and Stoke Charity, both in Hants. The cusps of these windows were also filled either with a continuation of the particular border employed, or with small circles of white glass stained with such devices as " I.H.C." (the Greek initial letters of the name Jesus), or " M." (for Maria, Mary). Radiant suns, the badge of Edward IV, were especially popular as cusp fillings, but only occurred in windows glazed between 1461 and 1485. White or blue roses, the last being merely decorative, were placed in some Dorset churches.

Special mention should be made of the manner in which the Crucifixion was treated by the fifteenth-century glass painters. As a rule, this subject, whether in a " figure and canopy " or in a " quarry " window, was comparatively simple in treatment, being generally, though not invariably, placed in an east window, preferably that of the chancel, and so arranged as to fill three lights, though the window itself might consist of a greater number. The arrangement was nearly always the same : a central crucifix, with the Virgin Mary and St. John the Divine in attendance, one on either side, the remaining lights, if any, being filled with figures of other saintly personages, as at St. Catherine's near Bath, and Winscombe in Somerset (Fig. 35), both being four-light windows. At Great Malvern Priory Church, where the three lights of a nave north-clerestory window were filled with a late fifteenth-century Crucifixion, the arrangement differed, St. John supporting the swooning Virgin in

the left light, while the right one was occupied by
Longinus, the Roman centurion, with his axe and
scroll inscribed : " Vere filius dei erat iste " (" Truly
this was the Son of God "). The Saviour was almost
invariably represented as nude, except for a coloured
waistcloth, and fastened to the cross by three nails,
the feet being placed one over the other, and fastened
by a single nail, while the hands were clenched. The
cross was often of the tau or Greek T shape, without
any top part, but with a tablet or scroll lettered I.N.R.I.
always set over His head. These letters, it may be
explained, stood for " Iesus Nazarenus, Rex Iudæorum "
(" Jesus of Nazareth, King of the Jews "), the title
set up by Pilate's orders. If the window were of the
" figure and canopy " type, a few accessory details
were often introduced into the central panel, notably
white-robed winged angels, hovering with chalices to
catch the blood as it streamed forth from the Saviour's
wounds, the sun and moon (in allusion to the darkness
which accompanied the Crucifixion), while on the
grassy plot whereon the crucifix was set up a human
skull was frequently depicted to indicate Calvary
(the Place of a Skull), supposed to be explained by an
early tradition that when the cross was erected, Adam's
skull was discovered. These accessory details were
usually lacking in the " figure on quarry " windows.
The figures of St. Mary and St. John in the side-lights
were usually represented as standing with upturned
faces, the former with clasped hands, the latter perhaps
holding a book, while both were often depicted as
weeping. It must be remembered that the representation of the Crucifixion was particularly obnoxious
to the Puritan reformers of the sixteenth and seventeenth
centuries, on account of its connection with the Mass ;
and crucifixes were often demolished ; while the
attendant figures of St. Mary and St. John were less
offensive in their eyes, and so frequently escaped destruction.   For this reason, therefore, in quite a number
of crucifixion windows the central panel of the crucified

Saviour is either modern, as at Nettlestead in Kent, and Himbleton in Worcestershire, or very extensively restored, as in the east window of Bowness Church in Westmorland. Other churches, such as Gipping in Suffolk, and St. Cross in Winchester, possess figures of St. Mary and St. John depicted in attitudes which clearly show that they were originally designed to be the mourners in a Crucifixion window.

4. *The Jesse Window.*—These were much less popular in the fifteenth century, and only a few have survived. In principle of design they agreed very closely with those of the previous century, but were less spirited in treatment. The vine stem was green, white, or orange, according to taste, the leaves and fruit being coloured, while the figures, clad in robes of various colours, and identified by their names on labels, were set within loops of the vine. The backgrounds of the panels so formed were red or blue. Occasionally the figures were arranged in pairs, as in a Jesse window of about 1460 at Margaretting in Essex (Fig. 36).

Mention should also be made of the very remarkable glass in the Beauchamp Chapel of Warwick Church, glazed in 1447 by John Prudde of Westminster, King's Glazier to Henry VI (see Chapter III, p. 30), at the cost of the executors of Richard, Earl of Warwick, the price paid being the high one of 2*s.* per foot (see Chapter II, p. 20). These windows, seven in number, seem to have been originally filled with figures of prophets, patriarchs, and saints : the two former, who wore peculiarly shaped hats and held inscribed scrolls, being placed in the side-windows, while the east window (now partly filled with fragments, including portions of several prophets) contained " some very prominent piece of Marian symbolism, such as her Coronation," together with four saints, St. Thomas of Canterbury (Fig. 33), St. Alban, St. Winifrid, and St. John of Bridlington. This window also contained a series of small kneeling figures depicting the Earl himself, his two wives, and their children. With the exception of the portraits,

all the figures stood upon tiled brackets, the fronts of
which were inscribed with their names ; the backgrounds
being diapered with foliage and divided by white
strapwork into a series of small compartments, either
lozenges on red or squares on blue, each containing
alternately the badges of the founder of the chapel,
namely, the white ragged staff and the white bear with
yellow chain and muzzle.   There were no surmounting
canopies, the figures with their scrolls being set against
the backgrounds, as though in a " quarry " window.
All these figures were clad in the richest colours in accordance with the terms of the contract (p. 19), their robes
being profusely ornamented with inserted "jewels," while
the four saints in the east window had bi-coloured haloes.

The treatment of the tracery lights was equally
elaborate.   In some windows were placed angels set
upon blue fields powdered with flaming yellow stars,
playing musical instruments, and dancing to the strains
they produced.[1]   In others red seraphim, standing upon
gold wheels, their backgrounds likewise of blue dotted
with gold stars, were singing plain-song music in honour
of the Virgin Mary ; those in the east window chanting
the " Ave Regina " (" Hail, Queen of Heaven ") from
the Sarum Antiphonale, while those in the side-windows
united in the antiphon " Gaudeamus " (" Let us re-
joice "), which was used on the Feast of the Assump-
tion.   The smaller traceries of the east window contained scrolls with the " Scripture of the Marriage of
the Earl," namely, the motto, " Louez Spencer tant
que vivray " (" Praise ye Spencer, as long as I shall
live "), in allusion to his wealthy Countess, who was the
heiress of the great Despenser family.   These scrolls
were placed on red or blue fields, painted to represent
clouds, and powdered with yellow flaming stars.[2]

[1] Some of these dancing angel musicians are illustrated in Westlake's
History of Design in Painted Glass, vol. iii.

[2] For further information, readers should consult Winston's *Memoirs of
the Art of Glass Painting*, pp. 326–41 ; and especially " The Music in the
Windows of the Beauchamp Chapel, Warwick," in *Archæologia*, lxi (1909),
pp. 583 et seq., by C. F. Hardy, where much of the glass is illustrated.

The tracery lights in this period formed a very important part of the Perpendicular windows, and should be carefully studied, as their contents often escaped almost intact when the main lights were destroyed. These tracery lights were filled with small figures of prophets, apostles, and saints, clad either in white and yellow, or in coloured robes, and placed against white, white and gold, or coloured fields, according to taste or circumstances. Sometimes they were surmounted by small canopies, more often they were merely set upon red or blue fields, usually arranged in a scheme of counter-change. Occasionally they were drawn in matt and stain on the greenish-white backgrounds themselves, as at Mottisfont in Hampshire (about 1480).

Angels were of frequent occurrence. As in the last period, they were of two distinct types : (1) those clad in white robes or albs, occasionally powdered with golden roundels, as in the east window of Ludlow Church, and frequently with apparelled amices (in stain) round their necks ; (2) those with bodies, arms, and legs covered by gold feathers, the latter type frequently wearing white scarves round their necks. Both types were almost invariably shown with curly yellow hair and white haloes, their wings varying in number from two to six, those of the feathered type of angel being sometimes composed of peacock feathers, as at Cirencester (Glos), Yarnton (Oxon), and Weobley (Herefordshire). These feathered angels were frequently depicted with hands raised in adoration, the palms turned outwards, standing upon a wheel (see p. 105). Examples of this treatment occur in Winchester Cathedral (north choir clerestory) and Yarnton Church, Oxon (Fig. 37).

Angels of both types were often shown as playing musical instruments, as at Hessett (Suffolk), Boughton Aluph (Kent), the St. Cuthbert window in York Minster, Cirencester Church (Glos.) (Fig. 39), and the Beauchamp Chapel of Warwick Church. The last-named series, with its angels singing from written music and dancing to the strains, has been described above (p. 121).

It should be pointed out that these series of angelic musicians did not represent " in any way a mediæval *orchestra* or band, who united to play in concert these instruments on which they were performers." Such combinations of instruments were unknown in the Middle Ages, when concerted music was in its infancy, and bands or *noises*, as they were then perhaps not inappropriately termed, were first formed of several instruments. These combined instruments were all of one kind, either all strings, or all shawms, or all trumpets and drums. Even as late as 1561, an orchestra performing interludes in the first English tragedy, *Gorboduc*, was divided into five distinct sections of violins, cornets, flutes, hautboys, and drums and fifes, each section performing separately.[1] The only exception to this divided use of instruments in combined performance was the common and popular union of the pipe and tabor.

Angels of both types were also frequently made to hold shields, charged with heraldic bearings, merchants' marks (usually drawn in black outline on white), or Passion emblems. The last-named, which were usually drawn in matt and stain on white, depicted the various instruments of Christ's Passion, such as the cross, nails, hammer, whipping pillar and scourges, the seamless coat, the dice, and so forth. Other tracery subjects included the symbols of the evangelists (sometimes set in roundels, sometimes on white or coloured fields, enriched with foliate diapers), heraldic badges or initial letters within foliage, or even grotesque monsters and heads. A figure of the Almighty, or perhaps a head of Christ only, was sometimes placed in the topmost light of all.

Apart from such stock subjects as the Annunciation or Coronation of the Virgin, pictorial scenes were not

[1] Galpin, *Old English Instruments of Music* (The Antiquary's Books, 1910), p. 274.

much used as tracery subjects. A few exceptions to
this rule did occur, notably in Great Malvern Church,
where the traceries of a north choir aisle window were
filled with the story of Joachim and Anne, together
with several incidents in the life of their daughter
Mary. The smaller tracery lights of these windows
were filled with half-length angels, shields, lion-faces,
grotesques, or foliage, usually in matt on white.

Heraldry was now very popular, and was therefore
often employed as a window subject both in tracery
and in main lights. As far as ecclesiastical glass was
concerned, the shields were usually of the " heater "
shape but shorter and not so pointed as those of the
previous century, while their surfaces were often enriched with diapering, rosettes being a favourite pattern.
Their " charges " were usually indicated in coloured
glass, both " insertion " and " abrasion and staining "
being freely practised, while the shields themselves
were now often divided up into more than four " quarters." Sometimes, however, the charges were merely
indicated in stain and matt on white, as in the Chapel
of the Vicars Choral at Wells. There was a change in
the royal arms about the year 1408, when " France
ancient," which had the blue field powdered with gold
fleurs-de-lys, was replaced by " France   modern,"
which had only three fleurs-de-lys, quartered with the
three English lions or leopards as before.

These shields in traceries, if not held by angels, were
either set upon a foliate background, or hung by their
" guiges " or armstraps from the branches of a small
conventional tree. Merchants' marks were often placed
upon shields in church windows, being usually painted
in black upon white. These devices, which generally
embodied the cross in some form or other, were used
by merchants as their distinctive emblems in marking
their bales of goods.

A great feature of this period was the introduction
into church windows of figures of the donors with their
wives and families. Although sometimes spoken of as

" portrait " figures, it was unlikely that, with the possible exception of royalty, the artists ever troubled themselves about attempting portraiture. Such figures were usually placed at the bottom of the window, the husband and wife sometimes kneeling face to face, the sons behind their father and the daughters behind their mother, as at Gresford in Denbighshire (see Fig. 31), and at Norbury in Derbyshire. Occasionally the two groups were divided one from the other by a central figure, perhaps that of the Trinity, as in the Blackburn window, All Saints', North Street, York, or formerly in the great north transept window of Canterbury Cathedral.[1] In other cases, they were all made to face towards the east, first, the husband with his wife, then the children behind, one or two figures in each light, if space were plentiful, or if only one family was being commemorated ; or, if the space was limited, in a compact group, as in St. Peter Mancroft Church, Norwich. In the case of royalty, the figures were shown kneeling at desks, placed beneath canopies of State, as at Little Malvern, or against tapestried backgrounds, striped with colour, as in the St. Cuthbert window in York Minster, or with the badges of the persons represented ; the whole often surmounted by gold cresting, the figures themselves being sumptuously attired, as befitting their high rank. In other cases the treatment of the persons represented depended greatly both upon their individual standing and upon the type of window in which they were placed. If in a figure, or a subject and canopy window, the donors might be placed in smaller niches beneath the main panels, against " seaweed " pattern backgrounds, as in Fromond's Chantry, Winchester College, or with panelling and brocaded tapestry above, as at Great Malvern, or with windows above hangings or panelling, as at Almondbury, in the West Riding of

[1] *Notes on the Painted Glass in Canterbury Cathedral* (London, 1897), p. 49 ; *Archæologia Cantiana*, vol. xxix (1911), Le Couteur, " Notes on the Great North Window of Canterbury Cathedral," p. 9.

Yorkshire (Fig. 38), and at St. Peter Mancroft
Church, Norwich. Again, they might be placed against
tapestried backgrounds, either of white or green, as
at Great Malvern, or of white and gold pomegranates,
as at Cirencester and Bledington (Glos) ; or even
against two-coloured stripes, as in the Roos portrait
panels at the foot of the St. William window in York
Minster. The figures themselves, or at least the parents,
were usually shown as kneeling at desks with open
books on them. But in a " figure upon quarry "
window the donors were almost always placed upon
quarries too, an exception occurring at Cirencester,
where a series of donors in a quarry window were set
upon white tapestried fields. Figures of persons to
be commemorated were occasionally introduced into
tracery lights, as in a window in the north choir aisle
of Great Malvern Priory Church, and in Hessett Church,
Suffolk. Sometimes, too, they were introduced into
the larger panels above, being then made to kneel
at the feet of a saint, as in the east window of Ross
Church, Herefordshire, and at Nettlestead Church in
Kent, the latter a " figure on quarry " window.

A very unusual treatment was that at West Wickham
Church in Kent, where a donor, Sir Henry Heydon
(about 1480), was represented as a skeleton kneeling
at a desk, with his plumed helmet near-by on the floor,
and a scroll inscribed " Ne reminiscaris domine delicta
nostra nec delicta nostrorum parentum " (" Remember
not, Lord, our offences, nor the offences of our fore-
fathers ").[1]

The costumes worn by these kneeling figures varied
greatly according to their individual station in life.
The usual civilian dress for men was a fur-lined gown,
reaching nearly to the feet, divided halfway up its
sides, and fastened at the waist with a belt, to which
hung a bag or purse (*gypcière*) (Fig. 40). On the
feet were pointed-toed boots. The hair was close-
cropped until the reign of Edward IV, when it was

[1] Nelson, p. 130.

allowed to grow long behind, being cut straight across at the neck and on the forehead. Ladies wore either a close-bodied dress, with long skirts and tight sleeves, or a looser dress with sleeves wide at the shoulders and tight at the wrists. The beautiful " side-less *cote-hardie,*" a close-fitting jacket with ermine or fur trimmings, was also worn by ladies of this period. Late in the century, heraldic mantles were often worn by ladies, as at Long Melford, Suffolk. The head-dresses varied greatly, from the simple kerchief and veil to the elaborate horned and butterfly types of the reign of Edward IV. The latter, which was introduced about 1475, consisted of an elongated framework of wire on which a white veil was stretched, the hair beneath being confined in a tight net or caul.[1] Armed donors usually wore complete plate armour, nearly all traces of mail having disappeared. That of the period of the Wars of the Roses was more elaborate, with fantastic elbow-pieces, but at the same time marvellously flexible. Heraldic tabards, at first sleeveless, later with short sleeves, the latter just covering the shoulders, were frequently worn over the armour towards the end of the century, as at East Harling, in Norfolk, and Long Melford, Suffolk (Fig. 38).

In texture the glass of this period was usually very smooth, and much thinner, and after 1450 or so the greenish tone of the white glass became much less marked. In quality the glass is apt to show signs of corrosion and decay, especially that made early in the century, due perhaps to the makers introducing an excess of impure alkali in an effort to obtain a thinner and so more brilliant type of glass.

[1] A good example is in the figure of Lady Anne Reinsforth at Long Melford, Suffolk: Nelson, plate 27, p. 210.

CHAPTER XI

THE RENAISSANCE PERIOD (1500–1550)

Towards the end of the fifteenth century English glass painting began to deteriorate in style, and to become stereotyped and commonplace both in ideas and execution. It may have been partly for this reason that Henry VII, soon after his seizure by conquest of the English throne in August 1485, began to invite foreign designers and craftsmen over to this country, men who could and did introduce fresh ideas and designs into English art. The result was that, as far as glass painting was concerned, all windows of the period 1500–50 must of necessity be divided into two distinct groups:

I. Those produced by resident foreigners, chiefly Flemings and Germans.

II. Those produced by Englishmen.

I.—It should be added that at first this introduction of foreign ideas made but little difference to architecture, and none whatever as far as the architectural design of windows and their tracery was concerned. Church windows were still purely " Perpendicular " in style, divided as before into tiers by stone transoms, their upper portions being subdivided into tracery. As the century progressed, however, there was a tendency with some architects to dispense with tracery, and to carry the lights right up to the top of the window, where they terminated in cinquefoiled heads, or sometimes in heads without any cusps at all.

It should also be pointed out that comparatively little of *original* foreign glass now remains in England,[1]

[1] A good deal of Continental glass of this and of other periods was imported into England by collectors during the eighteenth and early nineteenth centuries, such as the windows in the Lady Chapel of Lichfield Cathedral, the Jesse panels in St. George's, Hanover Square, and the fine collection formerly at Costessey Park, near Norwich. The Victoria and

by far the best examples being the twenty-eight windows in Fairford Church, Gloucestershire, and the twenty-five great windows of King's College Chapel, Cambridge. There are also considerable fragments in the choir of Winchester Cathedral, in Henry VII's Chapel, Westminster Abbey (chiefly heraldic, but including an imperfect figure of the prophet Jeremiah), and in Balliol College Chapel, Oxford. The famous east window of St. Margaret's Church, Westminster, is also of this period, but was considerably altered in the eighteenth century, probably by William Price, to fit it for its present situation.[1]

Both in King's College Chapel and Henry VII's Chapel the windows were filled with the scheme known as the " Story of the Olde Lawe and the Newe," a series of Old and New Testament types and anti-types (see Chapter V, p. 47). At Fairford the scheme was somewhat different, being intended to give " a pictorial representation of Christian theology. In that part of the church which is eastward of the dividing line of screens are set forth in picture-windows the facts, as taught by the Church, on which Christianity rests, and in the western part of the church are what may be called the inferences to be drawn from those facts, viz. the Apostles' Creed, the Church's teaching as symbolised by her ancient doctors, the Church's life as shewn forth by her saints and martyrs, and the final Judgment, the consummation of all things temporal."[2] Practically all foreign work painted in England during this period was divided into four distinct types, individual styles of course differing considerably one from another:

1. Figure and canopy windows.
2. Picture windows.
3. Jesse windows.
4. Quarry windows.

Albert Museum at South Kensington now contains a good collection of Continental mediæval glass, as does also Wilton Church, near Salisbury.

[1] The writer is indebted to Mr. J. A. Knowles for this information.

[2] F. S. Eden, *Ancient Stained and Painted Glass* (Cambridge Manuals of Science and Literature), p. 18.

1. *Figure and Canopy Windows.*—The figures in these
windows were slight improvements upon those of the
previous style, being rather better proportioned, while
a much greater knowledge of anatomy was displayed
in nude figures.   Hair and beards were drawn upon
the same piece of glass as the face, being " stippled "
out into long curling strands, sometimes grey, sometimes
stained ;   while the faces were strongly drawn with
heavy shading, and often with a certain rotundity and
fullness of features.   Haloes, when introduced, were
sometimes painted on the same piece of glass as the
head, but more often were coloured, and so leaded
on separately, a reversion to fourteenth-century practice.
Prophets were often shown as wearing coloured hats
of a peculiar shape with turned-up brims.   The
robes of these prophets and of the apostles usually
consisted of long tunics with deep sleeves, perhaps
confined at the waist by a girdle.   Over this was a
loose white mantle, the shoulders being sometimes
covered by a coloured tippet, as in the great east window
of Winchester Cathedral.   Saintly personages other
than the apostles, such as ecclesiastics, kings, or warriors,
were habited as became their respective rank, persons
of episcopal rank being sometimes vested in rich copes,
and were usually shown as holding each his or her
particular emblem, while their costumes were very
richly coloured.   Their draperies were still usually
arranged so as to contrast in colour with those of the
background, although there was no longer any attempt
at a strict scheme of counter-change, as was the case
in the previous century.

These figures were set within niches beneath coloured
groined or sometimes " scallop-shell " vaults (as in the
side-lights of the east window of St. Margaret's Church,
Westminster), with curtains or tapestried backgrounds
of various colours, green, blue, crimson, or maroon,
rising to their shoulders, often with a golden border at
top, and enriched by a large-patterned diaper.   Above
these curtains were frequently set windows, sometimes

round-headed, sometimes filled with Perpendicular traceries and mullions, all drawn in " matt " on white or bluish-grey glass.

The pavements on which these figures stood were tiled, usually in matt and white, though colour was sometimes used for this purpose, and the tiled patterns were much simpler than in the previous century. The bases varied very considerably, some being purely Gothic with three sides, and supported on small pillars, as at Fairford ; others were decidedly Classical, with " stained " flutings terminating in a pendant, as in a window of Temple Guiting Church in Gloucestershire. The scrolls bearing the names of these figures were usually placed on the fronts of the bases, or sometimes within it, as at Fairford ; or, again, might be held by a small angel set beneath an arch, as in a window of Henry VII's Chapel in Westminster Abbey. Such names were still inscribed in " black-letter " characters, usually in black on white, as in the two previous periods, but in some cases in stain picked out of black, as in one or two pieces of inscription preserved in windows of Winchester Cathedral.[1] In some cases, names, with other lettering, were painted on the borders of robes, as at Fairford (in the clerestory), Winchester Cathedral, (great east window), and Temple Guiting. Apostles and prophets usually held long scrolls curving over their heads and inscribed with Creed sentences in the one case and with parallel texts from the Old Testament in the other (see Chapter V, pp. 44, 45).

The surmounting canopy work was also typical of the period, being as a rule somewhat coarse and heavy, with deep shading, quite lacking the silvery tone of fifteenth-century work. Here, too, the design varied very considerably, some canopies being decorated with rounded turrets terminating in domes and pinnacles, both enriched with panelling, or pierced on either side

[1] In the westernmost window of the south choir aisle, which is half blocked by a transeptal chapel ; and in a scrap panel made up in an east window of the north transept.

with ornamental saltires, examples of both types being found at Fairford ; while other canopies terminated in coloured roofs, or in crocketed arches filled with colour, as in the choir aisles of Winchester Cathedral. Others, again, were markedly classical in type, these last being decorated with little naked cupids or amorini, or with festoons of foliage, grotesque heads, and the like, all drawn in matt and stain on white, as in a window of Basingstoke Parish Church. Occasionally canopy work was carried through more than one light, as in the great east window of Winchester Cathedral (ruined by " restoration " in 1852). Canopies, whatever their type, were usually placed upon plain fields of ruby, green, maroon, crimson, or blue, generally without any scheme of counter-change.

The supporting shafts of these canopies were fre- quently decorated with spiral stripes like those on a barber's pole, or with a diaper pattern of ornamental lozenges, all drawn in matt or in stain and white. The yellow stain of this period was often of a coarse orange tone due to " over-firing," and was laid on carelessly without much attempt to keep it within its outlined limits.

2. *Picture Windows.*—It is important to note that these foreign designers were inspired, not by the miracle plays, but by the great painters who flourished in this century, and whom they were trying to imitate, or even to rival, as far as was possible with glass and pigments. The picture windows that they produced were therefore very elaborate, often extending across two or more lights without any regard to the intervening mullions. Thus at Fairford, the whole upper five main lights of the great east window were filled with the Crucifixion, surrounded by a crowd of soldiers, Pharisees, and women, with hovering angels attending upon the Crucified Saviour, while the west window of seven lights was entirely de- voted to the Last Judgment. The figures, too, were frequently divided by the mullions, a flying angel being thus carried into two lights. The patterned blue and

ruby backgrounds disappeared, being replaced by plain blue of varying shades, upon which landscapes with trees, hills, and fields, buildings such as Gothic cathedrals or castles, and even rivers winding away between grassy banks, could be represented in matt and stain, as at Fairford, King's College Chapel, and in the Chapel of the Vyne in Hampshire.

These scenes receded in perspective, often reaching high up the lights and ending in clouds and sky painted on the blue, with birds circling and flying. Interior scenes were also elaborate and spacious; if of a church, often showing arcades, vaulted roof, and traceried windows, as at Fairford; or if of a domestic nature, having tiled floors, panelled walls, and perhaps furniture, with possibly even a vista of other rooms, all carefully painted in matt and stain both upon white and coloured glass. The architecture illustrated in these interiors was sometimes Gothic, as at Fairford, sometimes decidedly Classical, as in King's College Chapel (Fig. 41), where are "columns, friezes, architraves, and ornaments of the Renaissance, the cupids of Classic art mounted on fanciful steeds above the architraves, bearing the long festoons of garlanded leaf and flowers peculiar to this period; interiors, of which every detail contradicts the figures of mediæval architecture, are represented in perspective behind the Gothic mullions."

The figures in these pictures differed in one or two respects from those in the canopy windows, notably in the fantastic female head-dresses associated with sixteenth-century Flemish art, while the armour worn by military figures was often of a decidedly classical type, sometimes painted on blue glass enriched with stain, as in a window of Basingstoke Church. Haloes were sometimes flattened out as though drawn in perspective, a detail inspired by the "ring of light" treatment so often seen in the paintings of the Italian Masters. In other cases saintly personages were represented without a halo, as in the window depicting the

Unbelief of St. Thomas in King's College Chapel (Fig. 41). Outlines were no longer determined by the leadwork, faces and other details being often painted on the backgrounds, while it was a common practice to paint several heads of a group upon one piece of glass.

Canopies, if introduced at all into these picture windows, were comparatively simple, often consisting of little more than a very depressed arch carried across two or three lights, and surmounted by small spirelets, as in some of the windows at Fairford, where Gothic feeling predominated throughout; or suspended in mid air without any supporting shafts at all, as in Basingstoke Church and the Chapel of the Vyne about three miles distant.[1]

Another type of pictorial treatment was that in the east window of Balliol College Chapel, glazed in 1529 at the cost of Dr. Laurence Stubbs,[2] which, though foreign work, seems to have been based upon English principles of design. It was filled with a series of small panels arranged in tiers after the manner of fifteenth-century picture windows, but without any explanatory inscriptions. Each picture was set beneath a very depressed arch, some of Gothic type, others Classical, in each case painted upon pale-coloured glass. The backgrounds were plain blue throughout. The figures have the " flattened in perspective " type of halo, the armour and costume being apparently Gothic rather than Classical.

Explanatory inscriptions were no longer placed beneath these pictorial panels, but in King's College Chapel the central light of each of the twenty-four five-light side-windows contained four figures of "messengers," either prophets or angels, each holding a long curling scroll (Fig. 41). These scrolls bore Latin

---

[1] The glass in Basingstoke Church filling one window originally formed part of the glazing of the Sandys aisle of the Holy Ghost Chapel that stood in the Town Cemetery near-by. The glass in the Chapel of the Vyne is very similar.

[2] This refers to the old chapel, destroyed in the last century. The glass is preserved in the new one.

texts, taken for the most part direct from the Bible (the characters themselves being still " black-letter "), intended to explain one of the four pictures in that window.   Thus the Fall of the Manna (the Old Testament type of the Last Supper) was explained by " Panem de celo præstitisti eis : sapience 16," for " Thou didst send them bread from heaven. [Book of] Wisdom [chapter] 16 [v. 20]."   This part of the work was carelessly done, and contained many errors.   At Fairford there were neither " messengers " nor explanatory inscriptions at the foot.

3. *Jesse Windows.*—These still occurred, but were less popular.   In principle of design they agreed with earlier types, but differed considerably in detail, being more florid and decorative.   The figures were very richly clad, and often half-length only, being made to emerge from great floral cups of white and stain, the foliage and fruit being treated in the same colours, and the whole placed upon coloured fields.   Good examples of sixteenth-century Jesse trees remain at Llanrhaiadr in Denbighshire, and Dyserth in Flintshire (Fig. 42), while there are fragments of another in a window of St. James's Church, Bury St. Edmunds.

4. *Quarry Windows.*—These were of comparatively rare occurrence, so far as ecclesiastical glazing was concerned.   The aisles of Henry VII's Chapel seem, however, to have been glazed in this manner, each of the very many lights being filled with lozenge-shaped panes bearing such devices as H. R. (Henricus Rex), H. E. (Henry, Elizabeth), the portcullis, and the crowned hawthorn bush, the Welsh dragon entering into the design of every H.   The larger openings each contained a single shield or heraldic badge, but in neither case does there seem to have been any decorative border to the lights.   Other devices found in sixteenth-century quarries were initials held together by " true lovers' knots," Tudor roses, lilies, or a root of three daisies, the last in allusion to Margaret Beaufort, mother of Henry VII.

Traceries.—As in the previous century, traceries were filled with single figures of apostles, saints, and angels, usually treated in like manner to the larger figures in the main lights below. Sometimes, however, they were merely placed on bases and set against white or coloured backgrounds, as in the west window of Henry VII's Chapel. Angels were frequently introduced, being now of one type only, namely, clad in loose white robes, cut rather low in the neck, and usually with two wings only. These wings were often of two colours, the inside being of one colour, the outside of another, but not barred in colour as in the fourteenth century. Such figures were frequently represented as holding shields charged with Passion emblems, heraldic devices, and Royal monograms (Fig. 43), the last-named of the same type as those in the quarries, and, like them, drawn in matt and stain. The shields themselves, frequently held by their straps, were either of a flattened and broadened " heater " shape, or else of a peculiar ornamental type with top and bottom rolled up and cut into foliage designs. Regal heraldry of this period included several devices not hitherto found. These were the crown in a hawthorn bush, in allusion to the finding in a hawthorn bush of Richard III's golden circlet after Bosworth (August 22, 1485) [1] ; the portcullis, the white and red Tudor rose, either half white and half red, or red superimposed upon white ; the pomegranate sometimes halved and joined to a half-Tudor rose, and occasionally the white rose of York, the last in allusion to Elizabeth, daughter of Edward IV, whose marriage with Henry VII ended the Wars of the Roses. The smaller openings were filled with angel heads, half-length angels, heraldic badges, labels inscribed with the donor's motto, conventional foliage in white and stain, and so forth.

Heraldry was very popular in this period and also

[1] Not the regal crown of England itself, as is popularly supposed. Richard III merely wore a plain golden circlet round his helmet to indicate his royal rank.

very elaborate, both " insertion " and " abrasion and
staining " being practised, while coloured enamels,
which began to make their appearance towards the
end of this period (see p. 139) were also used to indicate
the charges on a shield. On the other hand, diapered
fields became less frequent. The shields themselves
were of various forms, and sometimes bore a large
number of " quarterings," while they were frequently
placed within green wreaths ornamented with coloured
roses, and ribbons set at intervals, or with roundels
containing heads at the sides. Royal shields were
usually encircled by the Garter, as were those of the
Bishops of Winchester, the Prelates of that Order.

The figures of donors so popular with English designers
were but rarely introduced into these foreign windows,
the very few examples being chiefly of royalty, as in
the Chapel of the Vyne in Hampshire, and in the east
window of St. Margaret's, Westminster, the latter
formerly in a private chapel. In the former case the
figures each occupied the central light in the lower half
of a three-light window, kneeling at a desk with his or
her patron saint standing behind, the central person,
King Henry VIII, kneeling before an altar, at the back
of which was a seated figure of Christ beneath a canopy.
In the St. Margaret's window the figures of Henry VIII
(not Prince Arthur, as is sometimes asserted) and
Catherine of Aragon kneel in niches at the sides, their
patron saints being placed above them.

The shading of this period was usually, though not
invariably, very coarse and heavy, being bold and deep
but perfectly transparent. It was first laid on in a
wash over the whole surface, and then " worked up "
by tapping and dabbing it with stiff hogshair brushes,
wiping it out in places so as to obtain high lights.
Hence as a rule the windows of this period lack that
golden shimmer and silvery transparency which was
the glory of the Perpendicular style.

II. *The English Glass* of this period calls for very
little comment, being in effect a poorer and decadent

type of fifteenth-century design, and embodying in its style several ideas copied from those found in the foreign work. The foliate backgrounds were usually retained, the draperies were richly coloured and heavily shaded, while the stain was of a marked orange tone. Both figure and picture windows were of the same type as before, though in the latter the canopy was sometimes dispensed with, each picture being then merely surmounted by a half-figure of the Almighty emerging from clouds, and perhaps attended by angels playing musical instruments, as in the Magnificat window of the north transept in Great Malvern Priory Church. The explanatory inscriptions in these picture windows were retained, being frequently in English, as at Greystoke in Cumberland.

Quarry windows were still popular, differing little from those of the fifteenth century, although more carelessly executed. An unusual treatment was that in St. Neot Church in Cornwall, where a number of figures on quarry grounds were each surmounted by tall and very clumsy embattled canopies, some of decidedly late fourteenth-century type (possibly taken from old cartoons purchased second-hand), the whole resting upon shafts.

Figures of donors were still of frequent occurrence in sixteenth-century English glass, being set as before at the foot of a window, kneeling in prayer at desks, sometimes with invocatory inscriptions on wavy scrolls issuing from their mouths, and twisting about over their heads. The heads of these donors were sometimes painted on the background and not surrounded by leadwork, as at St. Winnow (Cornwall), an idea copied from the foreign designers.

The costume worn by these kneeling figures was that of the period, the usual civilian dress for men being a long robe lined with fur and reaching to the feet, with wide sleeves, and encircled at the waist by a girdle from which hung a purse or *gypcière*, and sometimes a rosary. Women usually wore a pedimental or " kennel "

head-dress brought to an angle above the forehead
with long side-lappets falling on to the shoulders. The
dress was long and close-fitting, with square collar
and turned-back fur cuffs, while the girdle was loosely
clasped in front of the body with a long pendant terminating in a tassel or a scent-box (pomander).

Armed or knightly donors were now clad in plate,
but with a chain-mail skirt reaching halfway down the
thighs, while the feet were encased in large squared or
rounded toed " sabbatons." A short heraldic tabard
was frequently worn over the armour ; ladies of title
wearing an heraldic mantle over their dresses, as at
St. Winnow (Cornwall) and Dauntsey (Wilts).

In texture the glass of this period was usually very
smooth and thin, the quality being also very good.
The painting, however, was often carelessly executed,
so that it flaked off through insufficient " firing."
Towards the end of this period a new method of colouring glass was introduced, by which a variety of colours
could be obtained and painted on white glass. The
process, usually described as " enamelling," was simple,
merely consisting of crushing pieces of coloured glass
to as fine a powder as possible, mixing that powder
with some fusible medium, and then painting it on to
white glass, afterwards " firing " the piece so treated.
The heat of the kiln burned away the medium, at the
same time attaching the powder to the glass, with the
result that a thin film of colour, or, if need be, of several
colours, could be painted on to the same piece of white
glass. This method had, however, several serious
drawbacks. One was that the applied colour, especially blue, had a marked tendency to flake off, leaving,
of course, an unsightly patch, while the thin quality of
glass necessary to display to the full these applied
colours, coupled with the fact that it became unnecessary to outline the figures in leadwork, resulted,
in the seventeenth century, in the downfall of good glass
painting.

CHAPTER XII

FROM THE REFORMATION TO THE CIVIL WAR (1550–1640)

As might be expected, the Reformation and the resulting complete change in religious opinion effectively put a stop to practically all glass painting of a religious nature; such works, indeed, were now deemed " superstitious," and too often were either taken down or smashed (see Chapter XV). For the remainder of the century, therefore, the glass painters devoted themselves to producing heraldry and similar devices, although about 1575 a few small roundels containing religious subjects were painted for private dwellings (see Chapter XIV). At first the heraldic work was good in design and execution alike. Both " abrasion and staining " and " insertion " were freely practised, the glass varying in thickness, and the shields themselves being of several shapes. But side by side with this came the increasing use of enamels, and a growing tendency to use this medium in place of the more tedious methods of the older style. The result was that much of the heraldry produced both during the second half of the sixteenth century and early in the seventeenth was painted in colour upon a white surface, often placed within an oval surrounded by a decorative frame of scroll-work with grotesque faces, or animals terminating in pilasters, foliage, and the like, all drawn in matt and yellow stain, or perhaps in matt, stain, and coloured enamels. The date and, sometimes, the name of the bearer of the coat were placed at the bottom of the panel.

The seventeenth century, with its gradual evolution from Gothic to Classical architecture, at first made little difference to the glass painters, who during the earlier years continued to produce heraldic work as before. But about 1630 an attempt was made to revive Gothic architecture, while at the same time there was a return to the production of religious subjects as window designs. This revival of pictorial glass painting seems to have been largely due to Archbishops Abbot and Laud,[1] who encouraged several Dutchmen, among them Abraham and Bernard van Linge, to come and work in England, employing them about the glazing of their chapels, such as that of Abbot's Hospital at Guildford, and doubtless inviting others to do the same. Much of their work still remains in Oxford college chapels, notably at Wadham (1613–22), Lincoln (1629–31), University (soon after 1639), Queen's, and Balliol, while Lincoln's Inn Chapel in London, Lydiard Tregoze Church in Wiltshire (Fig. 44), and Messing Church in Essex, all retain some glass of this period.

In principle of design most of these windows agreed fairly well with those of the previous century, an important difference being that enamels now played a very much larger part in their colour schemes, while there was an ever-increasing tendency to dispense with leaded outlines and lead panels up in small rectangular panes. The adoption of enamels in preference to pot-metals was due to necessity rather than to choice. As already explained (Chapter I), much of the coloured glass used in this country was made in France and imported. The French glass makers of the seventeenth century were largely Huguenots who were being steadily driven from home by religious persecution, while in 1633, as retribution for the opposition offered to the armies of Louis XIII by the Duke Charles IV, a decree was issued that the whole of Lorraine (one of the chief glass-making centres) was to be laid waste, an act of vengeance duly carried out.[2] The result was that the

---

[1] F. S. Eden, *Ancient Stained and Painted Glass* (Cambridge Manuals of Science and Literature), p. 120.

[2] "Henry Gyles, Glass Painter of York," by J. A. Knowles, *Walpole Society*, vol. xi (1923). [*Antiquaries Journal*, vi (1926), p. 29.]

glass painters, who were, however, comparatively few
in numbers, had to eke out their supplies of pot-metal
by using enamels wherever possible, and, as will be
seen in the next chapter, had finally to set to work to
make pot-metals for themselves.

The work produced by the Dutch glass painters may
for convenience be divided into two distinct classes:

1. Figure windows.
2. Picture windows.

1. *Figure Windows.*—The figures in these windows
were well proportioned, but somewhat clumsy, some
being habited in long gowns with loose coloured mantles,
others wearing a jacket or tunic reaching to the knees
with close-fitting leggings or long hose beneath, the
colours being rich, with heavy folds of shading.   This
part of the work was usually executed in their pot-
metals, the figures themselves being outlined by the
leadwork.   Faces and all flesh tones were generally
delineated in reddish or muddy-brown enamels, but
occasionally in grey, painted in either case on white
glass.   The eyes were delineated in pale blue or white,
the iris itself being blue, while lips and cheeks were
usually tinted with brick-dust red.   Hair and beards
were either brown, grey, or stained, being sometimes
long, the latter cut to a point, " cavalier " fashion.
Haloes were circular or oval, sometimes flat, sometimes
leaded on in perspective.   Such figures might be placed
within niches with coloured curtains at the back and
traceried windows above, as in some of the Lincoln's
Inn Chapel windows, and in the side-windows of Lincoln
College Chapel, Oxford; or might be merely set against
scenic backgrounds with blue sky above, all drawn in
grey matt, stain, and coloured enamels, as at Lincoln's
Inn Chapel and Wadham College, Oxford.   The bases
varied very considerably in design, some being Gothic,
others decidedly Classical.   Their fronts were enriched
in some cases by shields executed in thin pot-metals,
in others (when supporting apostles or prophets) with
Creed sentences or Old Testament texts in Latin,

executed in Roman lettering (which had by this time replaced "black-letter"), as in the side-windows of Lincoln College, and in the south windows of Wadham College. The surmounting canopies, when present, were largely Gothic in feeling, but, as a rule, of no great height. They were executed in matt and stain on white. It should be added that, with very few exceptions, only apostles or prophets were represented in these Dutch figure windows; also that, though the donor's name, and sometimes that of the painter of the glass, together with the date, were often introduced at the base, there were no invocatory inscriptions.

2. *Picture Windows.*—These were by far the most popular with the Dutch enamel men. They were of two types: (1) Those with a series of pictures each contained within a single light, or even two in a light, as in the east windows of Wadham and Lincoln College Chapels; (2) those extending through more than one light, and even occupying an entire window, as in the chapels of Queen's and University Colleges, and in Christ Church, Oxford.

In either case the type of workmanship was nearly always the same. The personages represented, who were habited as in the figure windows, were drawn on thin pot-metals of brilliant colouring, and outlined in leadwork. Occasionally, however, enamels were used to delineate figures, as in University College Chapel, where a series of eight pictorial windows was almost entirely executed in enamels, pot-metals being used for one or two figures only. All scenic effects were obtained by the use of enamels, matt, and stain, the last-named varying very greatly in tone. The design was partly helped out in leadlines, and partly leaded up in squares. The subjects were taken from both Old and New Testament incidents, as at Queen's College, Oxford; sometimes arranged as type and anti-type, as in the east window of Lincoln College Chapel, although without the connecting "messengers." The lives of the saints were no longer drawn upon for window

subjects in England, and almost the only departure
from scriptural pictures was that at Messing Church,
Essex, where the east window represented six of the
Seven Works of Mercy.

Explanatory inscriptions, usually Latin texts, were
occasionally introduced, being executed in black Roman
type on white, set beneath each panel, as in the east
window of Lincoln College Chapel.

Perhaps the glass depicting Jonah beneath the
gourd in the west window of the north aisle of the
nave in Oxford Cathedral may be taken as a fair
example both of style and of colour-scheme (Fig. 45).
Jonah, clad in a blue robe with red mantle over, both
executed in pot-metals, is seated in the left-hand corner,
overshadowed by the luxuriant but somewhat gloomy
dark-green foliage of the gourd, among the branches
of which appear golden bell-like fruits. Above is the
scorching sun, whose rays beat fiercely down. In the
right-hand light is seen the city of Nineveh with its
harbour and shipping at the bottom, and the city
piling itself ever higher and higher upon the steep
hill, with its brown houses, bluish roofs, touches of
greenery, and fair, purple hills beyond.

The traceries of these Dutch windows were usually
filled with angels or other figures, standing or seated,
and holding shields, sometimes oval, sometimes of the
broadened "heater" type. Such figures might be
made to fill the entire light, or might be surmounted by
small canopies. Angelic figures of this period have
coloured wings (usually two in number) and robes.
Occasionally pictorial subjects were introduced into
traceries, as at Wadham College, Oxford. The smaller
openings were filled with cherub heads, foliate devices,
coats-of-arms, and the like.

The kneeling figures of donors, so popular in pre-
Reformation glass, were not placed in these windows,
but Oxford Cathedral retains a standing figure of
Robert King, last Abbot of Oseney Abbey and first
Bishop of Oxford, vested in a jewelled cloth-of-gold

cope over a white rochet, wearing a tall gold mitre, and holding a pastoral staff.   This window was the work of a Dutch artist.

The English work of this period, of which there is very little, may be described as a parody of the Dutch glass.   Perhaps the best-known examples are the north windows of Wadham College, representing prophets, painted in 1614 by Robert Rudland for the foundress, Dorothy Wadham, and the sepia windows in the ante-chapel of Magdalen College, Oxford, put up in 1635 by Richard Greenbury.

The former were executed chiefly in very dirty, washy enamels, some pot-metals being used for draperies. The figures stand on grassy bases with inscribed archi-tectural panels beneath, and the backgrounds are scenic.   The Magdalen windows, eight in number, are filled with a series of saintly personages, some of very uncommon occurrence, such as Wenceslaus, Theodosia, and Euphemia.   These figures, of a very heavy type with coarse puffy faces, were drawn in grey on white glass and leaded up in squares.   They stand on bases lettered with their names in Roman capitals.   There are no canopies and no scenic backgrounds, clouds being depicted above and behind their heads.   The traceries are filled with angels.

In texture the glass of this period was thin and smooth, while its quality was very good with but little trace of corrosion.   The outbreak of the Civil War in 1642 put a stop to all glass painting, the Dutchmen leaving England ; and with the exception of a few repairs, and perhaps a little heraldic work of a domestic nature, nothing more was done until the Restoration of the Monarchy.

CHAPTER XIII

FROM THE CIVIL WAR TO THE GREAT
EXHIBITION (1660–1851)

As might be expected, the reign of Puritanism with its violent antipathy to anything in the nature of church decoration wrought sad havoc with all forms of ecclesiastical art (see Chapter XV, pp. 159–62). It was not to be wondered at, therefore, that with the Restoration of the Monarchy in 1660 and the re-establishment of Episcopacy, only a few scattered glass painters remained to carry on as best they could the glorious traditions handed down to them by the past. Moreover, even these few craftsmen were struggling with almost insurmountable difficulties, for the destruction of the Lorraine glass factories thirty years before now left them with little more than matt and stain plus a few dull enamels wherewith to express their ideas of design. It was indeed due to the indomitable courage and perseverance of such men as Henry Gyles of York that we owe present-day glass painting,[1] and it is not to be wondered at if under such circumstances (to which must be added the general indifference of the times) the artistic standard of work produced was not a high one.

By the middle of the eighteenth century, however, more interest was taken in the subject, with the result that a greater number of craftsmen were in business designing and painting windows, often of considerable size. The chief men of this period were the three Prices (William senior, William junior, and Joshua),

[1] See "Henry Gyles, Glass Painter of York," by J. A. Knowles, vol. xi (1923) of the Walpole Society's publications.

William Peckitt of York, and Francis Edgington of Birmingham, while there were several smaller firms.

The medium in which all these men worked was for the most part the enamel process supplemented by matt and stain, the latter being now used in every imaginable shade, the whole painted on thin white glass. Pot-metals of a kind were also in use, especially about the middle of the eighteenth century, when several firms succeeded in making them. These coloured glasses, which included blue, red, maroon, and green, were very thin and brilliant, not to say gaudy and glaring, especially the blues, while the ruby was often streaky and irregular in surface, a curious throw-back to the early fourteenth century. In many cases, however, flashed ruby was not obtainable, and the designers had to do the best they could with the substitute of white glass turned red by repeated applications of stain, each with its own " firing."

The style now in vogue was largely Classical, although many traces of Gothic feeling still remained.

All ecclesiastical windows produced from 1660 to 1800 may for convenience be divided into two groups :

1. Figure windows.
2. Picture windows.

1. *Figure Windows.*—The figures of this period were, as a rule, tall and clumsy, arrayed in voluminous robes often of a semi-classical type, consisting of a mantle of one colour over a tunic or gown of another. They might be executed in thin gaudy pot-metals, as in the west window of Westminster Abbey (1735), or those on the north side of New College Chapel, or purely in enamels, as in the " Reynolds " window (1777) in the west window of the same chapel, executed by Thomas Jervais from cartoons made by Sir Joshua Reynolds. Faces and flesh tones were drawn sometimes in grey matt, sometimes in reddish enamels, painted in either case on the backgrounds, the faces being often of a wrinkled fleshy type. Hair and beards were grey, brown, or stained, according to taste ; haloes when

introduced being stained, and sometimes drawn in
perspective. These figures, whatever their composition, were usually leaded up in squares or rectangular
panes. Occasionally, however, they were outlined
in leadwork as in earlier periods, e.g. in the west window
of Brasenose College Chapel, Oxford. The backgrounds
usually consisted of squares of grey, heavily shaded
at one side or the other as though to indicate the shadow
cast by the figure. Canopy work and bases were sometimes introduced, either somewhat grotesque attempts
at Gothic, or frankly Classical, as in the great west
window of Westminster Abbey ; in either case drawn
in heavy matt and stain, the bases being sometimes
inscribed with the names of figures, executed chiefly in
block capitals, although " black-letter " was occasionally used for this purpose. The figures of this period
rarely included more than Old and New Testament
characters, such as patriarchs, prophets, and apostles.

2. *Picture Windows.*—In general type these may be
described as somewhat feeble parodies of those produced
by the seventeenth-century Dutchmen, and like them
were executed both in pot-metals and in enamels. They
differed, however, in being usually leaded up throughout
in squares, with the possible exception of heads, which
were sometimes outlined in leadwork (Fig. 46), as
in the Presentation in the Temple window at Oriel
College Chapel, Oxford, painted in 1767 by William
Peckitt of York. The backgrounds, too, were much
simpler, frequently consisting of yards of uninteresting
grey smear, although architectural interiors of a Classical type, or landscapes surmounted by pale blue sky,
were sometimes attempted, as in St. Andrew's Church,
Holborn, and Oriel College, Oxford. Tracery lights,
if any, contained such devices as heraldry, scroll-work,
interlaced triangles (emblematic of the Trinity), flowers,
or cherub heads, the last being of a fat, puffy type.
The name " Jehovah " in black Hebrew characters
on a glory of gold rays was sometimes placed in a
tracery light.

Dedicatory Latin inscriptions were occasionally introduced, being placed across the foot of a window, set out in Roman type. The date of the work and name of the artist were often given, as in Oriel College Chapel.

The heraldry of this period was usually of very poor design, being executed either in pot-metals or enamels, the latter having a marked tendency to flake off. The panels if large were leaded up in squares, as in the west window of Westminster Abbey, and in the east windows of both aisles of St. Andrew's Church, Holborn ; if small, they were painted in enamels within ovals or other shapes, surrounded by decorative borders, and usually bearing the name of the person commemorated upon a label beneath.

With the nineteenth century came a return to the mosaic principle of design, and an increasing desire upon the part of designers and of craftsmen to do better. Their early attempts were, however, very feeble, being chiefly poor copies of thirteenth-century work executed with execrable materials. Here and there were examples of fairly good design, notably the remarkable windows in North Stoneham Church, Hants, with shields placed upon ground-glass quarries, each enriched with a stained rosette, the whole within coloured borders. A still more noteworthy work was the modern copy, made between 1821 and 1828, of the original glazing of Winchester College Chapel (see p. 56), which, although utterly indefensible in itself, was, as far as craftsmanship was concerned, one of the most excellent pieces of glass painting that had been executed since the Reformation (Figs. 47, 48). " Then, just in the nick of time, came Charles Winston, the barrister, to whom modern English glass owes its very existence. An amateur of glass, possessed of insight and intelligence, he began at the beginning, instituting an inquiry into the nature and composition of the early materials, and, for the time being, leaving the question of design to look after itself. In conjunction with two well-known

glass makers, he produced the ' antique ' glass in use
at the present day, an excellent material, and made
better in England than anywhere else in the world." [1]
Thus, given proper materials, designers were encouraged
to proceed, and although for the remainder of the
century there was, and with some firms is still, a marked
tendency to turn out " trade stuff," based for the most
part upon Perpendicular designs, the art may now be
said to be as fully and firmly established and as well
understood as it was in the heyday of English mediæval
glass painting.

[1] Drake, *History of English Glass Painting*, p. 104.

CHAPTER XIV

SECULAR AND DOMESTIC GLAZING

ALTHOUGH but comparatively few mediæval secular buildings have retained their ancient glazing, it is well to remember that prior to the Civil War, especially during the fifteenth and sixteenth centuries, this beautiful form of art was employed as frequently for secular and domestic buildings as for ecclesiastical, varying in style and in costliness according to the individual building for which it was designed.

At first only royalty or the very highest of the nobility could afford to have coloured glass placed in the windows of their residences, but by the fourteenth century it began to be in greater demand, as is shown by more than one reference to it by contemporary writers, such as Chaucer.

The earliest examples extant consist probably of a few shields of late fourteenth-century work, now set in a staircase window of New College, Oxford, but once forming part of the hall glazing. In their original setting they would have been placed on quarry fields, one in each light, the whole within simple borders.

During the fifteenth and early sixteenth centuries coloured glass was in great demand for secular and domestic buildings of all classes, even small country rectories, such as that of Buckland in Gloucestershire. For the most part the secular glazing of this period was not of an elaborate nature, consisting, indeed, largely of quarries, either square or lozenge-shaped. The subjects on these quarries included such devices as rebuses, mottoes, sprays of foliage or flowers, animals, and birds. The last-named were especially popular

as quarry subjects, and were often shown as performing
quaint antics or carrying weapons, ringing hand-bells,
walking on crutches, and other occupations of a like
kind. They were frequently represented with little
scrolls bearing either English or Latin inscriptions
issuing from their beaks, sometimes of a sacred character such as " In nōie [nomine] Iesu " [" In the name
of Jesus "] at Buckland Rectory, Gloucestershire[1];
sometimes humorous such as, " Who blameth this ale ? "
held by a tit girded as a cellarer ; or " We must pray
for the fox," uttered by an owl ringing a bell ; which,
with other quarries of a like kind, probably brought
from some private dining-hall, are now in a window of
Yarnton Church, Oxon[2] (Fig. 51).

In the centre of such quarry lights might be inserted
a small circle or roundel, usually divided from the
field by an ornamental frame of some kind, drawn in
matt and stain on white, as in some glass from a merchant's house, now in Leicester Museum (Fig. 49).
Later on, in the sixteenth century, the border designs
were taken from natural foliage, such as sprays of
roses or lilies, drawn in matt and stain upon blue, or
picked out of matt on a white field, as in the Tudor
House (now Museum), Southampton.

The subjects in these little circles were drawn, as
a rule, from daily life, and included such scenes as the
Labours of the Months ; Harrowing, Sowing, Weeding,
Pruning, and Harvesting being especially popular
(Fig. 50). Scriptural subjects were also introduced,
as well as figures of the saints, or very occasionally
incidents from their lives. Whatever the subject,
the picture was drawn in matt and stain on white, the
figures being habited in like manner to those in contemporary glass of the larger windows.

Heraldry, too, played a very large part in secular

[1] *Transactions of the Bristol and Glos. Archæological Society*, vol. xlv
(1924), pp. 71–85.
[2] Bouchier, *Notes on the Stained Glass of the Oxford District* (Blackwell,
Oxford), p. 99.

and domestic glazing. It was exceedingly popular, as by this means people were enabled to display their family history, connections, and marriages. Badges (Fig. 51) and rebuses, or, if the owner were in trade, merchants' marks, were exhibited in this manner, as in the hall of John Halle, Salisbury.

How highly this form of display was valued may be inferred from the lines that Shakespeare puts into the mouth of the returned exile, Henry Bolingbroke (*Richard II*, Act III, Scene 1) :

> " . . . you have fed upon my signories,
> Dispark'd my parks and fell'd my forest woods,
> *From my own windows torn my household coat*,
> Razed out my imprese, leaving me no sign,
> Save men's opinions and my living blood,
> To show the world I am a gentleman."

Occasionally, if the person commemorated did not possess a coat-of-arms, it was the practice to use the goods wherein he dealt or the implements of his trade as a shield-charge. A good example of this " trade heraldry " appears in a window of the Westgate at Winchester, where is some fifteenth-century glass brought from the old Guildhall. One of these shields bears " Two gold candles with twisted butts in saltire " for Richard Kente, *a candlemaker*, while a second is charged with two *grozing-irons* in saltire, the owner, Henry Smart, being evidently a glass painter by trade (see Chapter II, p. 12).[1]

The shields themselves varied considerably in shape, especially in the fifteenth and sixteenth centuries. The charges on them were indicated in coloured glass, just as in ecclesiastical glazing. Occasionally such shields were placed between animal or bird " supporters," as at Ockwells in Berks, or held by angels, as in a window of the King's Head Hotel at Aylesbury, Bucks. Sixteenth-century heraldic glazing was fre

---

[1] Le Couteur, *Ancient Glass in Winchester* (Warren & Sons, Winchester, 1920), pp. 136–7. [These may be the arms of trade-gilds to which the persons belonged. See Chapter III, p. 28, and Plate VIII.]

quently set within ornamental wreaths of the type
described above (Chapter XI, p. 137). Such shields
were usually set upon fields of quarries, sometimes
arranged so as to alternate with diagonal labels bearing
mottoes, as at Ockwells, and in the hall of John Halle
at Salisbury, the whole light being set within a border,
although this last feature was not always introduced.

Figures were of comparatively rare occurrence, being
employed chiefly in the great window of a Guildhall,
as at Coventry, where the north window of St. Mary's
Hall is filled with nine large figures of kings, each clad
in armour with a coloured mantle over, and set against
a patterned background striped with M's, the whole
beneath a canopy. The traceries of the west window
of Boston Guildhall (Lincs) are filled with the Twelve
Apostles.

The glazing of a chapel, whether private or semi-
private, was, of course, of a more ecclesiastical nature.
It might consist of heraldry, or figures of saints and
apostles in quarries, as at Browne's Hospital, Stamford,
or even of scenes, as at the Vyne in Hampshire, Hen-
grave Hall, Suffolk, and formerly at Compton Wyn-
yates, Warwickshire.

During the course of the sixteenth century an important change took place in secular glazing, namely,
the adoption of a white glass transparent enough to
be seen *through*. The result was the disappearance
of the thick quarry work and the substitution of comparatively clear panes. These were leaded up into a
large variety of geometrical patterns, usually with a
shield-of-arms set within an oval, square, or lozenge-
shaped coloured panel for centre. Such shields agreed
more or less in type with those described in Chapter
XII, p. 144.

Besides heraldic works, little pictorial roundels
were very popular, "most of these being imported
from France and the Low Countries. . . . Their subjects
were drawn from all conceivable sources, secular fables
and legends being mixed with religious or family

histories in the most heterogeneous manner. Subjects
from the Apocrypha are frequent—the Story of Susanna
and the Elders being perhaps as common as any." [1]
These pictures were delineated in matt and stain in
white, the workmanship varying very greatly. They
were, however, readily distinguishable from English
work by reason of the many foreign characteristics·
both of dress and scenery introduced into them, while
their backgrounds were often quite as elaborate in
their way as the large scenic windows, towers, castles,
and trees, being etched in delicately by means of tracing
pigment. Moreover, as a general rule, they lacked
any ornamental borders.

The seventeenth century with its general adoption
of coloured enamels saw the revival of quarries, although
not on any extensive scale. This time the designs
were executed in colours and very delicately drawn,
the artists being for the most part Dutchmen. The
subjects on these quarries were very varied, and included badges, or even whole coats-of-arms, birds,
plants, sprays of foliage, or bunches of fruit, initials,
and such-like devices. Little roundels executed in
coloured enamels and containing scriptural scenes were
also popular. These usually bore rhyming and other
inscriptions in Dutch, sometimes with the name of
the householder, or even of the artist himself, the date
being generally included as well.

Heraldry was still very popular, the shields being
set for the most part within ovals and surrounded
by coloured borders, and the name of the person so
commemorated was often given together with the
date. Portraiture was sometimes attempted, busts
of persons being drawn in tracing pigment on white
glass within ovals or other shapes, sometimes surrounded by wreaths of foliage. Examples remain in
several Oxford colleges, notably at Magdalen, Wadham,
and Brasenose. Very few private chapels retain seven-

[1] Drake, *History of English Glass Painting* (Werner Laurie, 1912),
p. 78.

teenth-century glazing, an exception being that of
Abbot's Hospital at Guildford, glazed about 1620
with scenes from the lives of the patriarchs, the glass
painter employed being one of the Dutchmen working
in England about this time (see Chapter XII).　After
the Restoration of the Monarchy in 1660 and during
the eighteenth century coloured glass became less
popular in secular and domestic buildings.　Most of
the work executed was heraldic, together with such
subjects as small sundials (Fig. 52) and mottoes.
These designs were usually executed in matt and stain
supplemented by a few dull enamels, though pot-
metals were occasionally employed for the purpose.
The shields, which were of various shapes, were surrounded by foliage or ornamental devices, the whole
within an oval bordered by a thin band of colour.　Good
examples of this type remain at Barnard's Inn near the
Inns of Court, and the east window of Lincoln's Inn
Chapel is filled with eighteenth-century heraldry.
Larger windows agreed closely in type with ecclesiastical
work of the period, the design being no longer indicated
by leadlines, and all such work was generally dated.

CHAPTER XV

THE HISTORY OF DESTRUCTION

IT is a popular fallacy that most of the destruction both of ancient painted glass and of other forms of mediæval art that formerly adorned our cathedrals and parish churches was carried out during the Civil War, either by " Oliver Cromwell " or by the troops under his command. It is, of course, quite true that lamentable destruction was wrought during that unhappy period by soldiers of the various Parliamentary armies, but it is unfair to lay the blame entirely upon them, for, as history shows, infinitely greater damage was caused by the ignorance, carelessness, and indifference of the clergy, churchwardens, and architects of the eighteenth, nineteenth, and even of the twentieth centuries.

Even in pre-Reformation times much glass was destroyed largely by the rebuilding of yet older churches, notably at York Minster, where the great Norman church of the eleventh and twelfth centuries was entirely pulled down and rebuilt between 1240 and 1423, its windows being glazed afresh, with the result that practically the whole of the magnificent twelfth-century glazing of the earlier building was destroyed, a few odd panels only being kept, and used chiefly to repair gaps as they occurred in the new ones. Nor was care always taken of painted glass when set up, for in 1404 Robert de Braybroke, Bishop of London, was compelled to denounce those who profaned his cathedral (Old St. Paul's) by playing at ball or other unseemly games both within and without the building, *breaking the beautiful and costly painted windows, to the amusement*

of spectators [1] ; while in 1501 much damage was done
to the painted glass of Lincoln Minster by the arrows
and cross-bow quarrels shot at them by the servants
of the Dean (George FitzHugh).[2]

Enormous quantities of rich painted glass were
destroyed at the Dissolution of the Monasteries between
1536 and 1539, when numerous magnificent churches,
many of cathedral size, were either pulled down at
once or, having been stripped of their leaden roofs,
were allowed to fall to pieces by degrees. In a few
cases the townspeople succeeded in purchasing the
whole or a part of a monastic church for purposes
of parochial worship, or an abbey church was made the
cathedral of a new diocese, as at Gloucester, Peterborough, and Chester. In either of these cases the
painted glass windows would be sold with the building
and so saved for the time being. In a few other instances windows were saved by being purchased and
moved to some parish church, notably at Morley Church,
Derbyshire, which was enlarged in 1539 to receive a
considerable quantity of glass brought from the cloisters
of Dale Abbey in the same county.[3] But in the great
majority of cases the glass perished with the church,
fragments often coming to light centuries later during
the course of excavations.[4]

Much damage was also done to painted glass windows
by the Protestant Reformers, both under Edward
VI and Elizabeth, despite an attempt upon the part
of the latter to stop by Proclamation "the breaking
doune and defacing of any image in glasse windows in
any church, without consent of the Ordinary, . . .
offenders being liable to be committed to prison without
baile to await trial at the next coming of the Justices." [5]
Despite this injunction, great havoc was wrought by

[1] Purey Cust, *Walks Round York Minster*, p. 132.
[2] Nelson, p. 43.
[3] Nelson, pp. 69–72.
[4] At Shaftesbury Abbey in Dorset no less than three cartloads of glass
fragments came to light during excavations.
[5] Nelson, p. 44.

such uncompromising prelates as Horne of Winchester (1560–79), Jewel of Salisbury (1560–71), and Parkhurst of Norwich (1560–75).   Of the first it was well said that he " might never abyde aunciente monuments, actes, or deades, that gave any light of godly religion," [1] and he certainly lived up to his reputation.   At Durham Cathedral, where he was Dean from 1551 to 1553, he caused practically all the painted glass to be destroyed, while at Winchester his reforming zeal was such that in addition to doing great damage in the cathedral, he caused both Chapter House and Cloisters to be pulled down for the sake of their leaden roofs.   Not one single church in the whole county of Hampshire to-day possesses a perfect window of ancient glass; indeed, very many of them have not a scrap of that form of decoration.   Bishops Jewel and Parkhurst were less destructive, the latter chiefly waging war upon representations of God as an old man.

During the first half of the seventeenth century there was a steady growth of Puritan feeling in the country, despite the efforts of churchmen such as Laud, which now and again manifested itself in open outrages, such as that committed in 1632 by Henry Sherfield, Recorder of Salisbury, who, being offended by the pictures in a Creation window in St. Edmund's Church of that city, broke them with his staff.   For this offence he was severely punished by the Star Chamber.[2]

The outbreak of civil strife in 1642, followed by the rapid rise to power of the Puritan party, was responsible for widespread damage being done to cathedrals, colleges, and churches.   Some idea of the feeling prevailing at this time may be gathered from a petition signed by 12,000 " Weamen of Middlesex."   " We desire," it says, " that prophane glass windowes, whose super- stitious paint makes many idolaters, may be humbled and dashed in pieces against the ground ; for our conscions tells us that they are diabolicall, and the

[1] *Rites of Durham* (Surtees Society, 1903), p. 77.
[2] Nelson, p. 45.

father of Darkness was the inventor of them, being the
chief Patron of damnable pride." [1] In 1643 and 1644
Ordinances were issued by the Lords and Commons
assembled in Parliament for the utter demolishing,
removing, and taking away of all monuments of super-
stition and idolatry (such as all crucifixes, crosses, and
all images and pictures of any one or more Persons of
the Trinity or of the Virgin Mary), while Commissioners
and Visitors were appointed to see the law put into
effect. The spirit in which these " godly thorough
reformations " were carried out is well illustrated by
the description written by Joseph Hall, Bishop of
Norwich (1641–7), of the desecration of that cathedral
in 1643 by a mob under direction of the Sheriff, one
Tofts, and of two City Aldermen, Lindsey and Greenwood. "It is none other than tragicall," he writes,
" to relate the carriage of that furious sacrilege, whereof
our eyes and ears were the sad witnesses, under the
authority and presence of Linsey, Toftes, the Sheriff,
and Greenwood. Lord, what work was here ! What
clattering of glasses ! What beating down of walls !
What tearing up of monuments ! What pulling down
of seats ! What wresting out of irons and brass from
the windows and graves ! What defacing of arms !
What demolishing of curious stone-work, that had not
any representation in the world, but only of the cost
of the founder and skill of the mason ! What tooting
and piping upon the destroyed organ pipes ! And
what a hideous triumph on the market-day before all
the country, when in a kind of sacrilegious and profane
procession all the organ pipes, vestments, both copes
and surplices, together with the leaden cross which had
been newly sawn down from over the green-yard
pulpit, and the service books and singing books that
could be had, were carried to the fire in the public
market-place ; a lewd wretch walking before the
train, in his cope trailing in the dirt, with a service
book in his hand, imitating in an impious scorn the

[1] Leslie Waterhouse, *The Story of Architecture* (Batsford), p. 181.

tune, and usurping the words of the litany used formerly in the Church. Near the public cross all these monuments of idolatry must be sacrificed to the fire ; not without much ostentation of a zealous joy, in discharging ordinance, to the cost of some who professed how much they had longed to see that day. Neither was it any news upon this Guild-day to have the cathedral now open on all sides, to be filled with musketeers, waiting for the mayor's return, drinking and tobacconing as freely as if it had turned alehouse."[1]

Another of these "Visitors" was William Dowsing, who "reformed" the East Anglian churches, and by virtue of a pretended Commission went about the country "like a Bedlam, beating down all the painted glass, not only in the chapels, but, contrary to order, in the public schools, college halls, libraries, and chambers."[2] This fanatic kept a diary of his proceedings (1643–4), of which the following extracts are typical:

"Sudbury (Suffolk). Gregory Parish, January 9th. We brake down 10 mighty great Angels in glass, in all 80.

"Stoke-Nayland, Jan. the 19th. We brake down an 100 superstitious pictures ; and took up 7 superstitious Inscriptions on the Grave Stones, *ora pro nobis*, etc.

"Somersham (Aug. 22nd.). A Cross in the glass, and St. Catherine with her wheel, and another picture in the glass in the church ; and 2 superstitious pictures in the window.

"Eye, Aug. the 30th. Seven superstitious pictures in the Chancel, and a cross ; one was Mary Magdalene ; all in the glass ; and six in the church windows ; many more had been broken down afore."[3]

In addition to the visits by Commissioners, several cathedrals, among them Lincoln, Chester, Lichfield,

---

[1] Geo. Lewis, *Life of Joseph Hall* (Hodder & Stoughton), p. 401.
[2] *Dictionary of National Biography*, William Dowsing, vol. xv, p. 407.
[3] Dowsing's Journal has been edited by C. H. E. White (Ipswich, 1885) and J. C. Wall (London, Church Printing Co.). An abridged edition has been published by Talbot & Co.

Peterborough, and Winchester, were sacked by the soldiers of various Parliamentary armies. Of Peterborough, we are told, the soldiers " were not kind to the cathedral and its surplice-furniture " [1]; while at Winchester Waller's troops pulled down the Renaissance chests containing the bones of many early Saxon kings which were set on the side-screens of the choir, and amused themselves by flinging them at the painted glass " so that the spoil done upon the windows will not be repaired for a thousand pounds." [2]   Much of the debris was afterwards gathered up and set anyhow in the great west window of the nave.

Much mischief was also done by Puritan ministers of religion, such as Canon Henry Jenkinson of Christ Church, Oxford, who " furiously stamped upon the windows of his cathedral when taken down, utterly defacing them," [3] or Richard Culmer, the Puritan Rector of Chartham in Kent, who smashed much of the painted glass in Canterbury Cathedral with a " whole pike." [4]

In a few cases windows were preserved by being taken down and concealed until better times came.   The Fairford glass is said to have been saved in this way ; also the three windows in the Chapel of the Vyne near Basingstoke, and the east window of St. Peter's College (Peterhouse), Cambridge, where the infamous Dowsing broke down " two mighty angels with wings, Peter on his kneies over the chapell door, and about a hundred cherubim, also divers letters in gold." At York, too, most of the glass both in the Minster and in the city churches was saved by the exertions of Lord Fairfax, himself a Yorkshireman, who was in command of the Parliamentary forces during the siege, and upon its

[1] Carlyle, *Oliver Cromwell's Letters and Speeches*, vol. i (vi of the Centenary Edition), p. 145.

[2] *Mercurius Rusticus* (ed. 1685), p. 149.

[3] H. L. Thompson, *Christ Church* (College Histories Series, London, 1900), p. 72.

[4] Culmer tells his own story in a pamphlet, " Cathedrall Newes from Canterburie " (1644). The part relating to the destruction of the glass is given in Woodruff & Danks, *Memorials of Canterbury Cathedral* (Chapman & Hall, 1912), p. 327.

capitulation accepted as one of the articles of surrender
the condition that cathedral and churches alike should
be protected from harm.

Throughout the eighteenth century, the era both of
non-resident clergy and of ignorant and indifferent
churchwardens, the miserable tale of destruction received numerous additions. Windows were now falling
to pieces for want of releading or even of simple repairs,
with the result that they became unable to stand wind-
pressure, and so collapsed or were blown out. This
fate overtook the fine glass of St. John's, Stamford,
(Lincs), of Fotheringhay Church in Northamptonshire,
and of all the south windows of Nettlestead Church
in Kent, the last-named being blown out by a storm
in 1763. In Hilton Church, Dorset, much painted glass
was destroyed about 1730 " by some idle persons." [1]

In some cases windows were stolen to decorate another
church, or even to enrich a private collection. A
particularly outrageous case was that of Tattershall
Church in Lincolnshire, where in 1757 almost all the
remaining ancient glass was given by the patron, Lord
Fortescue, to the Earl of Exeter, who removed it to
his own Church of St. Martin's, Stamford Baron, where
it exists, for the most part in a very jumbled condition.
The Tattershall parishioners very justifiably raised a
riot in an endeavour to prevent this scandalous spolia-
tion.[2] Another case of the sale of ancient glass occurred
at Bexhill, where a window full of figures of various
dates [3] was sold by the churchwardens to Lord Ash-
burnham, and by him given to Horace Walpole for his
famous villa at Strawberry Hill. After other wanderings,
it was finally restored to the Church in 1922. Instances
were not wanting of valuable ancient glass being cleared
out to make way for poor eighteenth-century glazing.
This happened at Merton College (the east window of

[1] Hutchins, *History of Dorset* (new ed., 1870), vol. iv, p. 357.
[2] *Highways and Byways in Lincolnshire*, pp. 387-8.
[3] The Homeland Association's *Handbook* (vol. 84): *Bexhill-on-Sea*,
p. 30, gives an illustration of the glass.

the choir) and at New College, Oxford, the latter in 1777, when the great west window was emptied of its gorgeous glass to make room for the panels designed by Sir Joshua Reynolds and executed by Thomas Jervais. During the "restoration" by Wyatt of Salisbury Cathedral in 1788 the greater part of the glass, both pictorial and grisaille, was cleared out by the cartload and emptied into the city ditch, after having been "beaten to pieces" for the sake of the lead. The spirit in which the work was carried out is well illustrated by the following letter,[1] written in 1788 by "John Berry, glazier of Salisbury, to Mr. Lloyd of Conduit St., London, 1788.

"SIR,
        "This day I have sent you a Box full of old stained and painted glass as you desired me to doe, which I hope will suit your Purpos, it his the best that I can get at Present. But I expect to Beate to Peceais [Pieces] a great deal very sune, as it his of now use to me, and we do it for the lead. If you want more of the same Sorts you may have what thear is, if it will pay you for the taking out, as it is a Deal of Truble to what a Beating it to Pecais his; You will send me a line as soon as Possible, for we are goain to move our glassing shop to nother plase and then we hope to save a great deal more of the like sort, which I ham
                "Your most Omble Servant
                                "JOHN BERRY."

Even when glass was suffered to remain it was often grievously maltreated. In Winchester Cathedral and Great Malvern Church the south choir clerestory windows were *whitewashed* over, the same thing happening to ancient glass at Fordwich Church in Kent.[2] Another favourite practice, and one unhappily still prevalent,

[1] Nelson, p. 48.
[2] Dr. Francis Grayling, *Kent* (County Churches Series), vol i, p. 26.

was to collect the remains of ancient glass from a number of windows, which had been glazed at different times by various glaziers, and to relead them up either in a jumble or in some sort of arrangement in one large window. Thus, in 1799 at Canterbury Cathedral, the great south transept window was filled up with twelfth-century figures from the choir clerestory, set beneath the original late fourteenth-century canopies, the whole bordered with debris of various dates, much of which was cut up into strips. This work was " selected and arranged with much care and industry by Mr. John Simmonds, one of the vesturers of this church, to whom the arrangement was committed by the Dean [Powys] and Chapter." [1]

In the nineteenth century things were little better, ancient glass being stolen, sold, or lost in abundance. In 1823 most of the glass in the east window of Norbury Church was sold to a Yorkshire family.[2] Much glass was lost by " restoration," as at Winchester College, where between 1821 and 1828 the whole original glazing of the chapel, inserted in 1393, was removed and re-placed by a careful modern copy (Fig. 50).[3] In this case the ancient glass had apparently become very corroded and opaque, so much so as to make its repair beyond the skill of the firm employed. The great east window of Ludlow Church in Shropshire suffered the same fate at the hands of the same firm in 1832.

Great damage was done by the " Gothic Revival " (from about 1850 and onwards), when architects laboured to make churches as uniform in style as possible, with the result that much valuable glass and other forms of mediæval art were ruthlessly swept away. Examples of these destructive restorations are numerous, minor ones resulting in the loss of ancient glass including Newington by Sittingbourne (in 1862) and Milton Swale

---

[1] *Notes on the Painted Glass in Canterbury Cathedral* (Aberdeen University Press, 1897), p. 44 ; Nelson, p. 117.
[2] Nelson, p. 49.
[3] Le Couteur, *Ancient Glass in Winchester*, pp. 69–71.

(in 1873), both in Kent[1] ; while in Exeter Cathedral a complete Decorated window which had been found in the Minstrels' Gallery was actually cut to pieces by the Chapter glazier to make coloured borders for his plain glazing.[2] Much glass has been lost by the insertion of new memorial windows. As late as 1882 it was seriously proposed to clear the great west window of Winchester Cathedral of its vast collection of ancient glass, itself a jumble of many dates, in order to insert a memorial to Bishop Wilberforce. The prompt intervention of Dr. Ridding, then Head Master of Winchester College, happily stopped this piece of vandalism.[3]

Even in this twentieth century the danger of damage to ancient glass is by no means past, for many incumbents and even architects seem ignorant of, or indifferent to, the priceless works of art entrusted to their care. Only a few years ago it was left to the Head Verger of one of our most famous cathedrals to forbid the removal from a window of several fifteenth-century heraldic badges to make way for modern glass; while there have been several other cases of small portions of ancient glass being taken out and left to lie about the church, or be leaded up in some other window for which they were not designed, or, worst of all, to be thrown away as " not worth keeping."

During the Great War of 1914–18 yet more damage was done. The seventeenth-century windows of Lincoln's Inn Chapel were blown in by a bomb explosion during a Zeppelin raid, with the result that two were destroyed for ever, and the others much damaged. In other places, notably at Westminster Abbey, St. Margaret's Church, Westminster, and at Great Malvern, the ancient glass was taken out and carefully packed away until the danger was past.

Happily there are now signs that the Church of

---

[1] Grayling, *Kent* (County Churches Series), vol. i, p. 29.
[2] Bishop and Prideaux, *The Building of Exeter Cathedral*, p. 147.
[3] Lady Laura Ridding, *George Ridding, Schoolmaster and Bishop* (London, 1908), p. 135.

England is at last awaking to the value of the great heritage entrusted to her care. Following the recommendation made in 1912 by a Select Committee of Lords and Commons that the State should take control of the cathedrals as national monuments, which ought to be protected by legislation from mishandling by incompetent custodians, the Archbishop of Canterbury promised that the ecclesiastical authorities would take the necessary protective measures. Accordingly a small committee, consisting of the Vicar-General, Sir Lewis Dibdin, and two Diocesan Chancellors, investigated the matter and suggested, among other remedies, the formation of expert advisory bodies in every diocese " for the assistance of the Consistory Court in architectural, archæological, historical, and artistic matters relating to churches as to which faculties are sought."

As a result of this recommendation Advisory Committees have been formed in the dioceses, consisting of the leading clergy, distinguished antiquaries, and eminent architectural and other experts. These Committees meet regularly and at frequent intervals to consider and report on the cases connected with faculties which have been submitted to them by the Chancellors ; while their advice and assistance are placed at the disposal of all incumbents, who avail themselves of them to an increasing extent. In addition there is a " Central Committee for the Protection of Churches," chiefly composed of delegates from each Diocesan Committee, which deals with questions referred to it by the Diocesan Committees, and with other cases which do not come within their scope.[1]

But it cannot be said that the present position is altogether satisfactory. In two dioceses there is still no Committee ; and in one or two others the system is still very little developed. Apart from this, these

[1] For more detailed information, readers are recommended to consult the Central Committee's Reports on *The Protection of our English Churches* (Oxford University Press, 1923, and the Press and Publications Board of the Church Assembly, 1925).

Committees, as at present constituted, are not strong enough : they can only advise and suggest. It is certain that they will have to be considerably strengthened, so that the present risk to some of our most precious national treasures, not only painted glass, but also other forms of mediæval art, may be prevented.

There are, of course, a few whose solution of the problem is to insist that all repairs of the ancient cathedrals and churches should be undertaken by the State. But apart from the undesirability of State interference in such matters, there is nothing to show that the work of preservation would be any more skilfully or sympathetically carried out if undertaken by a Government Department.

It is evident, therefore, that the responsibility should and must continue to rest with the Church authorities ; and it is for them to develop and work the system which the Church herself has set up. One thing is certain, that there is a great need for a more educated clergy—educated, that is to say, in the sense of understanding and appreciating the great and real value, both historical and artistic, of the treasures often entrusted to their care. To this end, therefore, it is desirable that all candidates for Holy Orders should have some regular instruction in the subjects of ecclesiastical architecture, archæology, and art ; nor should they be allowed to take Orders until they had satisfied a Board of Examiners, drawn from the Advisory Committees, that they had really acquired some such knowledge, and would be prepared to co-operate with them in safeguarding such treasures as might at any time be entrusted to their care.

CHAPTER XVI

THE PRESERVATION OF ANCIENT GLASS

IT may not be out of place in a work of this description
to offer a few suggestions as to the preservation and
restoration of ancient glass. With regard to its preservation, it is well to remember that atmospheric action
combined with antiquity will in time play havoc both
with the glass itself (see Chapter I, p. 9) and with the
leadwork in which it is set. Against the former evil
there appears to be no adequate defence; but any
damage to the leadwork is soon obvious by reason of
gleams of daylight, often quite minute, showing between
glass and lead. If this initial warning is neglected, the
next stage of decay is heralded by the slow inward
bulging of the panel or panels by reason of wind pressure,
which often causes the glass to crack or break. Finally,
if not taken in hand in time, one or two pieces of glass
will fall out, followed sooner or later by the whole of
the panel or even window being blown in and destroyed
(as in the case of the south windows of Nettlestead
Church, Kent), or at the best reduced to a fragmentary
condition.

It is therefore of the utmost importance to have
ancient glass carefully examined from time to time
by a glass expert, even if it has been releaded within
the last sixty years. If repairs or releading are found
to be necessary, the work should be entrusted to some
well-known firm of glass painters, and not to the local
glazier, who, however clever he may be at making
plain " quarry " lights, is often unable to distinguish
the right and wrong side of painted glass, and so sometimes replaces it with the painted side exposed to the
weather.

The question of restoration is perhaps more de-batable, and greatly depends upon individual cir-cumstances. Any attempt at rearrangement should only be undertaken if the work can be directed by antiquarian experts, and carried out by skilled crafts-men; otherwise further damage may easily be inflicted by loss of material, owing to the edges being cut in order to fit pieces to their new positions. For this reason it may be deemed best to relead windows exactly as before, replacing any lost pieces with plain white or greenish-tinted glass, the latter for preference (as in the west window of St. Mary Redcliffe Church, Bristol, a capital example of a careful and conservative restora-tion), though even then any glaring sheet glass should certainly be removed. A better method is, if possible, to fill any gaps with pieces of the correct shape and colour, care being taken to use the proper kind of coloured glass. Such inserted pieces should, of course, be plain, or at the most have only a light wash of pigment fired on to them, and should if possible be marked by the initials of the firm employed lightly scratched thereon. Heads, if cracked, should be " plated " if possible, that is to say, leaded between two pieces of white glass of the same shape, in order to avoid the insertion of leads across the features. Tracings should always be made of any fragments of inscrip-tions that may be found inserted, with the possi-bility in view of obtaining valuable clues to the contents of other windows long since destroyed; while, should circumstances allow, these pieces should be set at their right level, and not left inverted or reversed, as is too often the case. Moreover, where any two or three fragments of inscription can be definitely identified as having formed part of the same legend, they should be collected and set out in as nearly their original order and position as possible.

All alien fragments should also be carefully examined for the same reason, but should not be removed unless there is something better with which to replace them.

The practice of bordering a window with a strip of fragments of various dates is to be deprecated, as half the glass is frequently embedded in the cementing on the outer side. If such pieces do exist, they should be leaded into a scrap panel, and set as close to the eye as possible, not " skied " in tracery lights.

If several windows (each containing remains of its original glazing) need releading at the same time, it is a great mistake to remove the glass from all with the intention of making up one " scrap " window. To do this is to destroy a chapter or even a series of chapters in the history of that particular church. The few inches of border or the dozen or so of quarries enriched with running foliate patterns of early fourteenth-century work, the Yorkist suns and roses still lurking in the cusps of a Perpendicular window, the fragments of heraldic shields and badges remaining in tracery lights, or the debris of a pictorial series, perhaps with figures of donors beneath, will, if carefully releaded and re-placed *in situ*, often furnish the antiquary with more information concerning the history of the building or parish than he would obtain by weeks of research in other directions.

An important point to be remembered by anyone about to take charge of releading operations is that, if it is intended to make any changes in the arrangement of a window, the glass should be well and carefully *studied before it is taken down*. The expert should first make up his own mind as to his exact intentions, and then, having worked out his scheme, should go over it carefully with the chief craftsman of the firm to be employed, so making certain, not only that it is understood, but that it is practicable. To wait until the glass is out and upon the bench is a fatal mistake.

CHAPTER XVII

HINTS TO STUDENTS

ALTHOUGH each student will, no doubt, follow his or her own methods of studying ancient glass, the following hints may be of use.

1. It is advisable to equip oneself with a pair of glasses, the stronger the better (though even opera-glasses are not to be despised). Such glasses, whatever their power, should not be pressed against eyes or eyebrows, but held about half an inch away ; otherwise severe neuralgia may result. Those with weak eyesight would be well advised not to take up this line of archæology, while colour-blindness is, of course, a fatal bar.

2. *Where to find Ancient Glass.*—It is a safe rule to enter every church, whether old or new, together with any secular or domestic mediæval building that is accessible to the public. Of course very many ancient churches have not retained a vestige of their ancient glazing, while some modern buildings (such as St. Nicholas, Wilton, near Salisbury) are perfect store-houses of old glass. Should a church be locked, it is a good plan to walk round *outside*, paying especial attention to the tracery lights and cusped heads of windows, also to vestry and porch windows, which often contain interesting pieces removed from elsewhere in the building.

3. *How to examine Ancient Glass.*—The first thing is to determine its period, and in this the beginner will often find the type of window tracery to be helpful, although, of course, there are many instances of glass having been inserted in windows for which it was not

172

intended. Should the student be fortunate enough to
have a window full of ancient glass to examine, he
should first note its general characteristics, type, and
treatment of figures, canopies, backgrounds, borders,
and inscriptions, together with the heraldry, if any ;
not forgetting the glass in the tracery lights. He should
then concentrate upon one particular light (if in a figure
and canopy window) or one panel (if of a pictorial type),
and carefully analyse its contents, noting the manner
in which it is made up and put together, the treatment
of dress, headgear, face and features, background, and
other lesser details, and mentally compare each or
any with those of any other window that he considers
to belong to the same period.

Finally, he should endeavour to imagine how a figure
or a panel would look *if it formed the only piece of ancient
glazing left in a big window* ; how, for instance, the
figure would look if deprived of background, canopy,
base, and identifying label, and leaded up perhaps in
plain quarries. An expert is sometimes called upon
to identify and date a figure in this condition, and
to make a theoretical and (if he be a professional glass
painter) a practical reconstruction of a window from
little more than a figure, or a confused jumble of debris
of heads, and pieces of figures (as witness the reconstruction in 1870 of the east window of Windermere
Parish Church). If, on the other hand, the student has
but fragmentary debris to deal with (as, alas! is too
often the case), he must work backwards, and endeavour
in theory to reconstruct the panel or window as best
he may from what remains. Thus an Early English
lancet window, retaining a few fragments of grisaille,
would have been filled with the same type of glazing,
or if the foliage therein showed a tendency towards
natural treatment, such a window would probably
have contained a small pictorial panel or panels as well.
A Decorated window retaining fragments of coloured
borders, and quarry fields, with perchance the topmost
pinnacle of a canopy drawn on yellow pot-metal, can

be partially reconstructed in theory without undue difficulty. Again, the appearance of a radiant sun, or the letters I.H.C. or M. in stain on a white roundel, or a scrap of gold crown so painted as to show part of a white interior, set in the cusped heads of the main lights of a Perpendicular window, at once suggests that the window when perfect was of the "figure on quarry" type (see Chapter X, p. 116) ; while the radiant suns show that the glass dates between 1461 and 1485.

4. It is well to make detailed notes of the remains of ancient glass in each church visited, giving particulars of colours, dress or vestments, backgrounds, borders, and other details. If a sketch can be made, so much the better, while the date of the visit *and the condition of the glass itself* should also be noted, any damage being reported to the incumbent, or if (as is sometimes the case) he should prove indifferent, then to the General Secretary of the Central Committee for the Protection of Churches, Victoria and Albert Museum, South Kensington, S.W.7. Notes made on the spot may afterwards be written out in a larger book, so that in time the student will have amassed a quantity of information which may in years to come prove of the greatest possible value to antiquaries. It is also helpful, if one possesses any county maps, to mark thereon each church containing any ancient glass (however fragmentary or slight the remains) with a red or blue pencil. In this way a record of one's activities is gradually formed.

5. *In sketching ancient glass*, most people of artistic tastes will find their own appliances, but to beginners it may be helpful to say that water-colours such as Reeves's, or Winsor & Newton's, are the only satisfactory medium for colour work, while Reeves's White Bristol Board or Imitation Steinbach or Greyhound drawing-paper gives very satisfactory results. If pencil only be employed, it is necessary to make a note of the colours.

6. *In photographing ancient glass,*[1] one wants a stand camera, with, if possible, a swing back and rising front, which often have to be called into use when photographing glass at a height. A spirit-level to see that the camera is level and that the back is plumb is absolutely necessary, to ensure that the sides of the window are not out of the perpendicular, otherwise the photograph will be out of proportion. The camera must therefore be level and square with its subject. For plates an " Imperial Panchromatic " (desenitol backed) or an Eastman Panchromatic film with a K-three screen is desirable in order to secure the proper colour values, especially when there is a predominance of red or yellow, and to lessen the chances of halation or blurring of the high lights. With a little care no difficulty should be experienced in using Panchromatics, as long as a red light is not used in the dark-room. An ordinary flash-lamp with two thicknesses of " Paget Safelight " yellow paper and two of green over the bulb, used with discretion, will give quite sufficient light for the purpose.

For actual working, an average exposure of 15 or 20 minutes with F/22 stop, developed with pyro soda, and in such a way as to get all detail without too great a density, will give fine negatives suitable for enlargement. Be critical about focusing in order to secure uniform sharpness. In actual practice it is always well to secure a negative of the entire window, and then, if time permits, single panels or sections on a large scale.

The greatest trial to a " glass " photographer is (especially on the south side) the screen of protecting wire on the outside of a window, which is much more apparent on a bright day than on a dull one. Intervening lamps or chandeliers, or carved screens across the chancel, often cause difficulty, and here the photographer's own resourcefulness alone can help him. It is always advisable to carry plenty of string with one.

[1] I am deeply indebted to Mr. W. M. Dodson for this information.

In order to raise the camera, much can be done with four chairs (if a table from the vestry is not available) or with hassocks and books on the seats and bookrests to make the camera stand steady and level. Of course, everything should be tidied up afterwards and left as it was when work was commenced.

Those who only possess Kodaks and small cameras (if they have a plate back or film pack attachment) need not be disheartened, as art films can be obtained to fit all slides and screens to fit all lenses. If a small stop is used, and care be exercised in development, most satisfactory enlargements (at least to 8 × 6 inches) can be secured.

If time is short, it is often wise to ascertain *beforehand* whether permission is necessary to sketch or to take photographs, as in some places rules and regulations are very strict. In the case of a cathedral, any such inquiries should be addressed to the Head Verger, but for a parish church to the incumbent.

GENERAL INDEX

Abbot, George, Archbishop of Canterbury, 141, 156
Alemaygne, John de, of Chiddingfold, 6
Apocryphal Gospels, 50
Armour, 40, 63, 76, 92, 106, 127, 133, 139
Arthur, Prince of Wales, 37, 137
Aubrey, John, quoted, 25, 26

Backgrounds, of figures, scenes, and canopies, treatment of, 63, 65, 69, 70, 72, 81, 83, 85, 93, 103, 113, 114, 117, 121, 125, 126, 130, 132, 133, 134, 138, 142, 148, 154
Badges, 11, 117, 118, 135, 136, 153
Ball-flower ornament, 113
Bases under figures, see Pavements.
Benedict Biscop, 58
Benedictine habit, colour of, 46, 106
Berry, John, glazier of Salisbury, 164
Bible, Latin (the Vulgate), 50
Biblia Pauperum, 47, 49, 60
Black Death, 56, 97 note, 107
Black-letter inscriptions, 64, 100, 104, 112, 115, 131, 135, 143, 148
Borders of lights, treatment of, 64, 65, 67, 70, 71, 74, 76, 81, 87, 88, 89, 98, 100, 103, 118, 152
Bradeston, Thomas Lord, Constable of Gloucester Castle, 33
Brampton, John, 21
Burgundy, Lower, glass made in, 7
Butterfly head-dress, 127

Cable family of Frome, 117
Cæsarius of Heisterbach, Dialogue of Miracles, 52
Calmes (leads), 15
Canopies, 65, 82–84, 93, 98, 99, 102, 103, 112, 114, 116, 131, 134, 138, 143, 148
Cartoons for painted windows, 17, 18, 138, 147
Catherine of Arragon, 37, 137

Chamber, John, junior, of York, 26 note 3
Chartres, a centre of glass painting, 59
Chiddingfold (Surrey), glass made at, 6
Churches, appearance of English mediæval, 33
Cistercian Order and painted windows, 59
Contracts for painted glass, 19–21
Corrosion of glass, 9, 95, 107, 127, 145
Costume in glass, mediæval, 62, 106, 110, 111, 126, 127, 130, 133, 138, 139, 142
Cote-hardie, the sideless, 18, 127
Counterchange of colours, 71, 72, 85, 95, 98, 110, 113, 130
Crecy, battle of, 97
Cross-hatching of backgrounds, 73, 74, 79, 80, 100
Crown glass, 5
Culmer, Richard, Rector of Chartham, 162

Donors, figures of, in glass, 67, 77, 87, 92, 94, 100, 106, 124–126, 137, 138, 144
Dowsing, William, 161, 162

Edgington, Francis, 147
Edward I, 89
Edward III, 24, 92, 96
Edward IV, 118, 136
Ekworth, John, of Bridlington, merchant, 7
Eleanor of Castile, Queen, 89
Elizabeth of York, Queen, 135, 136
Emblems of the Apostles, 44, 45
—— —— Evangelists, 90, 91, 123
—— —— Passion, 123, 136
—— —— Saints, 42, 86
Enamels and enamelling, 137, 139, 140, 141, 142, 143, 145, 147, 148, 149, 155

177

Subjects represented in glass (*cont.*):
  Saints (*cont.*) :
    Thomas of Canterbury, miracles
      of, 69
    — Cantilupe of Hereford, Fig.
      20
    Wenceslaus, 145
    Werstan, story of, at Malvern,
      114
    William of York, life of, 52
    Winifrid, 120
    Samuel, 16
    Seven Deadly Sins, 55
    — Sacraments, 36, 54, 55
    — Works of Mercy, 36, 55, 90, 144
    Susanna, story of, 155
    Synagogue, figure of the, 65
    Te Deum, 55
    Trinity, 125, 160
    Virtues, the Cardinal, 65
Sundials in glass, 156
Surcoat, heraldic, 92

Tabard, heraldic, 127, 139
Tables of glass, 3, 5, 8
— whitewashed, on which designs
    for glass were drawn, 10, 12, 17
Tame, John, and Sir Edmund, of
    Fairford, 34
Templates, 10
Theophilus, treatise on glass paint-
    ing by, 12, 22, 59
Thornton, John, of Coventry and
    York, 48
Throckmorton, Sir Robert, 36

Tracery lights, subjects in, 56, 89–
    91, 100, 105, 121, 122–124, 144,
    145, 148
— — survival of old glass in, 104,
    122, 172, 173
Tyrrell, Sir James, 35

Utynam, John, glass manufacturer,
    6

Van Linge, Abraham and Bernard,
    141
Verrour (verrer), 25
— Robert le, of Colchester, 25
— Walter le, of York, 25
Vestments, ecclesiastical, 46, 75,
    93, 102, 106, 111
Vincent of Beauvais, 52
Vulgate, 50

Wadham, Dorothy, 145
Walpole, Horace, 1 note, 163
Walter le Verrour of York, 25
War, the Civil, 145
Wars of the Roses, 108
Warwick, Richard Beauchamp,
    Earl of (d. 1439), 19
Wilfrid, St., Bishop of York, 58
Windows, painted, origin of, 58
Winston, Charles, 149
Wykeham, William of, Bishop of
    Winchester, 16, 27, 104, 105, 106

York glass, 2
— school of glass painters, 26

TOPOGRAPHICAL INDEX